CONTENTS

INTRODUCTION

It was a slow realization of the potential. There was no particular moment in horticultural history when gardeners awoke to an appreciation of the exquisite beauty of the many and varied species that have come to be grouped together under the term 'alpines' or 'rock garden plants'. Certainly many whose natural homes are in rocky, high-altitude areas (including, of course, those of the Scottish Highlands), had been collected and transplanted to gardens, but the inherent problems in their cultivation were soon realized. They are plants of exacting habitats, as I shall explain later.

But the increase in foreign travel and the gradual attraction of the Alps and other mountainous areas for visitors and mountaineers in the early years of the nineteenth century prompted a greater specific interest in the possibility of cultivating alpine plants. It

Ramonda myconi **is at home in any alpine collection**

became apparent that some semblance of their natural homes might be the answer to alpine culture. Various crude attempts at building mountain-tops in lowland gardens ensued, particularly in Britain, and one of the earliest seems to have been created in a quarry at Fonthill, Wiltshire, around 1820. Others followed, often attempting to recreate entire mountains or even mountain ranges on a small scale. The Alps around Chamonix were recreated at Hoole House in Cheshire and planted with a range of alpine plants in the 1830s, but – rather typically – the whole was set in a garden of formal beds and, later, miniature Swiss chalets were added too. Other rock gardens included alabaster 'snow' on the mountain-tops and even afforded to visitors the opportunity of viewing the scene through telescopes.

By the end of the nineteenth century, however, serious alpine plant gardening gradually took over, to a large degree under the inspired guidance of Yorkshireman Reginald Farrer, who has earned the sobriquet 'the father of English rock gardening'. He was an outspoken character and utterly dismissive of the attempts to build the rock gardens of the time: 'the chaotic hideousness of the result is to be remembered with shudders ever after', he wrote. Subsequently, following Farrer's lead, rock gardens came to be built as replicas of small alpine habitats rather than entire mountains, and by building them of stone appropriate to the region in which the gardens were sited, carefully setting the rock in its natural bedding planes and not placing the whole in an incongruous surround, success slowly followed.

Even so, the more difficult alpine plants were and still are necessarily grown in special greenhouses where they can be protected from the vagaries of the lowland winter. Rock gardening on a grand outdoor scale has waned in recent years, largely because of the small size of most modern gardens, the cost of obtaining and transporting rock, and a growing consciousness among gardeners of the environmental damage that quarrying can bring about. Today, alpine gardening has never been more popular, but the plants are increasingly grown in alternative ways.

In this book, I describe all of the ways in which rock garden plants can be grown, discuss in detail the advantages and disadvantages of each, and give guidance on the year-round care of the plants. I then give my personal selection of the multitude of species and varieties that now exist, concentrating on those that will be most widely available and are least exacting in their requirements (some alpine plants thrive naturally in conditions, such as micro-habitats close to the melting snow of glaciers, that are all but impossible to replicate in lowland areas). I have indicated those species and varieties that have been given the Award of Garden Merit (AGM) of the Royal Horticultural Society. This doesn't necessarily mean you will like them or automatically succeed in growing them, but at least they have been selected by experts on the basis of careful trials as appropriate for cultivation in the garden.

The Alps are the home of many, but certainly not all, alpine plants

WHAT ARE ROCK GARDEN PLANTS?

Let me first dispel the notion that there is any difference between rock garden plants and alpines. The terms are interchangeable, although both are slightly inaccurate. Rock garden plant implies one that is grown in what has become known conventionally as a rock garden. However, as will become evident from the next few pages, this is but one way of growing them; it is simply the way that was employed when the plants first became popular during the nineteenth century and the name has stuck. Today, they are at least as likely to be grown in a container of some sort, in a raised hollow-wall bed, in a scree bed or in an alpine greenhouse. I shall look in detail at each of these methods shortly, but here I want to concentrate on the relevance of the alternative term alpine.

Self-evidently, alpine means something pertaining to the Alps, and while there are mountains in various parts of the world that have adopted the name (the Southern Alps of the South Island of New Zealand or the Australian Alps stretching from Canberra through New South Wales and Victoria, for instance), it is the familiar mountain range of southern Europe that everyone has in mind. Since this was the area first visited by the mountaineers who were the initial collectors of the local plant life, the name stuck. Subsequently, mountain ranges in other regions were visited, too: the Himalayas, Tien Shan, Andes, Rockies, Atlas and other mountain ranges of Africa, and many more. Today, there is scarcely a mountain that hasn't been climbed and no mountain range that hasn't been visited. Wherever mountaineers could go, plants were collected and brought home, generally as seeds, to be grown at leisure.

The Alpine Environment

It was then that gardeners began to realize the challenges that many of these plants offered. Planted in normal garden beds and borders, most failed, so people began to think about and examine the characteristics of the plants' native habitats to see how best these could be replicated. The soil in which alpine plants grow, by and large, was no great problem, but it did vary widely. It might be thought to be invariably stony, thin and free draining, and often it is, although small pockets of soil and humus may accumulate in sheltered spots that are very different from those only a few metres away on the exposed mountainside. Even thin mountain soils are often far from impoverished, however, and contain large amounts of dissolved mineral matter which offers valuable plant nutrients. The acidity or alkalinity (pH) of the soil varies hugely, depending on the nature of the underlying rock itself: the soil on a limestone mountain-top may have a pH of well above 8, that on a comparable granite mountain down to 4. Once all of these conditions are understood, nonetheless, they can generally be reproduced in an artificial compost, although I can generalize to the extent of saying that if you offer alpine plants a free-draining, gritty, soil-based compost with a pH around neutral, you will succeed in the majority of cases.

It was when gardeners came to consider alpine weather and climate that they began to understand some of the reasons for their early failures and some of the difficulties that had to be overcome. In the wild, alpine plants often experience widely differing extremes of temperature: both diurnally, between the scorching midday sun and the penetrating wind and frost of the night, and also seasonally, the mountain peaks commonly being baked in the height of summer but buried

Armeria maritima **is an example of a rock garden plant that grows on coastal cliffs rather than in mountains**

Many small varieties of bulb like *Narcissus* 'Peeping Tom' find a home in the rock garden

beneath snow for months on end in winter. Rainfall is very high but the air is in constant movement. Today, however, with a much greater understanding of the needs of particular plants it is possible to offer a selection such as those in this book, a choice of those most amenable to the conditions that prevail at lower altitudes. Once you have grown these, you may, like many before you, become addicted to alpine gardening and want to attempt some of the greater challenges; so, in due course, do let me know how and when you succeed with the likes of *Ranunculus glacialis!*

Plant Type

Finally, I must make one important point. An alpine plant is defined ecologically, by its habitat, not by its botanical relationships to other plants. Alpine plants represent a huge number of families and genera, many of which contain lowland species too. The form and overall appearance of an alpine plant is also dictated by its ecology. They are invariably small, compact, adapted to minimize water loss and prevent desiccation, flower close to ground level so that pollinating insects visiting the flowers aren't blown away, generally lack fragrance because that too is blown away, but are often brightly coloured instead. Some plants from other, less strictly mountainous areas, have developed similar features, and because they are often easy to cultivate and grow well in alpine gardens I have included a selection here.

There are very few true alpine annuals, largely because the alpine summer is too short to give annual plants very much of a chance of germinating, producing a seedling, growing to flowering size and setting seed again. However, a further reason that annual alpines aren't especially popular with alpine gardeners is that their sowing and subsequent removal creates disturbance of the many perennial species, and also because fast-growing annuals (which they must be) can soon swamp the entire bed, to the detriment of everything else that is there.

Gentian lutea **shows that familiar genera can yield unexpected species; it is neither a neat little alpine nor is it gentian blue**

ROCK GARDENS AND SCREES

I have already referred to Reginald Farrer, 'the father of English rock gardening', and his distaste for the rock gardens of his day. He was in truth quite specific and categorized rock gardens as 'almond puddings', 'devil's lapfuls' and 'dogs' graves', depending on what he felt they most resembled. I can empathize, because even today many, indeed the majority of, rock gardens are totally incongruous. I've seen creations in some of our great public gardens that look more akin to the sides of a Greek temple than anything geological. Yet a well and thoughtfully constructed rock garden can look magnificent, so don't let me dissuade you from having one; I ask simply that you do some homework first.

Building a Rock Garden

Before you lay any rock, you must create a soil environment that is appropriate. My preferred way is to dig out a hole to the approximate area of the proposed rock garden and lay old broken bricks, pieces of concrete or whatever other material is available to produce a well-drained base. Mix the soil removed with approximately equal volumes of very well-rotted leaf mould or similar plant compost and horticultural grit. If your soil is naturally acidic, choose an acidic, lime-free grit; if it is alkaline, choose an alkaline one. Replace the mixture and give it about two weeks to settle down.

You don't need to know any geology to build a good rock garden, but a little helps. It helps if you know the type of rock that occurs naturally in your area, because any rock garden you build should try to match it; and it helps to understand the way that a natural rock outcrop appears, because that after all is what you are trying to reproduce.

It's important to appreciate the difference between rocks that occur naturally in layers, called bedding planes, which reflect the way they were formed (often laid down in water), and rocks that occur massively, as great, apparently amorphous lumps. Many sedimentary rocks such as sandstones, grits and shales occur in layers, as do some metamorphic rocks like schists. Igneous rocks like granite, and a few sedimentary rocks like certain types of limestone, occur massively.

If you are constructing your rock garden with rocks that are more or less flat, in bedding planes, lay them with these layers parallel. Generally, you will find they look most attractive if the layers are dipping gently at a shallow angle rather than entirely horizontal or entirely vertical. Massive rocks are much harder to place convincingly unless they are very large, but look carefully at natural rock outcrops, take photographs if possible, and try to copy them.

It's important to ensure that you have created a range of habitats in your rock garden. Most alpines thrive best in

Creating a rock garden needn't entail a massive construction using huge rocks; small-scale rock gardens are very attractive

If a rock garden is to resemble a natural outcrop of rock, it is best done on a fairly grand scale

full sun but some do need varying amounts of shade, so be sure to position your rocks to create a few shady spots where these will thrive.

Please be careful in obtaining your rocks. You cannot simply trot out to the nearest hillside and hack off a piece. Stone can only come legally from properly approved commercial quarries, which tend to be a long way from where the stone is needed. Hence, it is pretty costly. There are some excellent artificial stones now available, however, and you will find that good, larger garden centres have a selection of real and artificial from which you can choose. Never underestimate the weight and use appropriate lifting equipment and help, or you could

seriously injure yourself.

Finally, cover all exposed soil with a layer of grit approximately 2cm (¾in) deep. This will help to maintain the moisture content and temperature of the soil at relatively uniform levels, will prevent soil (and any harmful organisms it contains) from being splashed onto the plants, and will enhance their appearance.

Building a Scree Bed

Look at the foot of many mountain slopes and you will see an accumulation of loose rocks, graded as they have rolled or slid down such that the largest are at the bottom and the smallest at the top. This is a scree. In

the early stages, a scree is in constant movement as more material is being added, but eventually, when most of the loose rocks have been washed down the mountain, the pile at the bottom becomes more or less stable. It is then that plants can begin to grow in it, and it is this environment that a scree bed seeks to emulate.

The initial soil preparation for creating a scree bed is the same as for a rock garden, except that it is much better to build it on a natural, gentle slope. Then, instead of embedding relatively large rocks in the soil, simply place a load of smaller, fragmented rocks over the top, raking and sorting them to match the gradation in size that occurs in a natural scree.

TROUGHS AND OTHER CONTAINERS

I have devoted an entire book in this series to containers (*Best Container Plants*) and in it I stress my long-held belief that any type of plant can be grown in a container; it is simply a matter of finding something appropriate. Generally, containers are used as an addition to more conventional garden plantings in beds and borders but, for reasons I have already indicated, alpines cannot be grown in normal beds and borders, and purpose-built rock gardens are not to everyone's taste or within everyone's means. Containers therefore have a uniquely special part to play in the cultivation of alpines.

There is no reason why you shouldn't grow alpines in any sort of container, provided you use an appropriate compost, but do bear in mind that they are inherently small, low-growing plants that won't make a huge impact in the garden as a whole. They need to be viewed at fairly close quarters for their beauty to be appreciated fully. Because they also tend to be plants that are relatively unchanged from their natural appearance (plant breeders haven't distorted them in the way they have roses and chrysanthemums, for example), they generally look best in a container that also appears relatively natural, or at least is made of a natural material.

Stone Troughs

For all these reasons, the stone trough has come to be recognized as the ideal container for alpines, best of all when raised above the ground and closer to eye level to create what is called a table bed. Stone troughs weren't, of course, invented for plant growing. They are hollowed-out lumps of rock that have been used for centuries to contain drinking water for cattle and horses, but once gardeners wanted them farmers chose to realize their assets and give water to their livestock in metal tanks instead. Demand, of course, outstripped supply and, while

A trough, either of real or artificial stone, is an ideal way to grow alpines on a small scale

A hollow wall offers an excellent environment for rock garden plants and brings them closer to eye level

stone troughs are still regularly seen for sale at garden auctions, the prices are now very high.

If you do want a trough for your plants and cannot find or cannot afford an original stone one, there are two options. Artificial versions are now available at a fraction of the cost, or you can create you own using, most simply, an old glazed sink as the base. Although any size and shape of sink can be used, the best are those that are relatively shallow; about 15cm (6in) deep is ideal. The glazed surface should be coated with a material called hyper-tufa, but it will bond better if the glaze is roughened first. Use an electric drill with a coarse carborundum disc, and remember to wear goggles when you do so, or 'paint' the surface with one of the adhesives used for car body repair. The hypertufa itself is a mixture of one part by volume cement, one part sharp sand and two parts moss peat, made with water into a thick, porridge-like mixture. Apply it to the sink with a mortar trowel, adding it in layers and leaving a surface texture like rough stone.

For growing alpines in troughs, I place a layer of coarse grit in the base and then use a soil-based potting com-post to which I add an equal volume of horticultural grit. Carefully arrange small rocks half-buried in the surface to add visual interest, although unlike in a larger rock garden it isn't really feasible to create much shade in a container of this size.

Hollow-wall Beds

Another 'container' option is to grow alpines in a raised, hollow-wall bed, although just as a stone trough looks much better than a terracotta one so a raised bed is immeasurably more attractive when built of stone than of brick. Do be sure that there is drainage at the base, however.

Whatever container you use, finally top it up with a layer of grit, just as recommended for rock gardens (see p. 8).

11

ALPINE HOUSES AND MEADOWS

The biggest problems in growing alpines relate to the clinging damp of the lowland winter. It is therefore simply to give added protection that many alpine enthusiasts prefer to grow their plants totally under cover.

The Alpine House

There is nothing very unusual or special about an alpine house. It is simply a greenhouse with no heating, but with some form of summer shading and with additional ventilation. If you think of it more as a giant cloche, you won't be very far wide of the mark. It really doesn't matter which type of greenhouse you use: wooden or aluminium, lean-to or span, glass to ground or raised on walls.

Your plants will be grown individually in small pots, ideally of terracotta rather than plastic. This, of course, gives you the opportunity to tailor the compost specifically to the needs of each plant; those that require highly alkaline conditions can be grown alongside those that need high acidity. There is nothing wrong with simply standing the pots on an open bench in the usual way. Nonetheless, you will obtain better results, and a much more attractive display, if they are sunk to their rims in a bed of grit, which will buffer any temperature fluctuations and also help to keep the moisture content of the pots fairly steady. A bench of grit and pots will, however, be very heavy, so it is well worth investing in very robust metal staging at the outset.

The Alpine Meadow

By definition, alpines constitute the flora of the mountains, but it's only when you see them in the wild that you realize that they don't grow solely in little pockets in rock crevices or among the loose boulders of a scree. There are vast areas, whole high-altitude meadows of the things.

But how do you go about creating an alpine meadow at low altitude and in limited space? I don't pretend that it's easy, but it can be done. There are two broad soil types in alpine meadows and you need to decide which one your existing soil most closely resembles. The first is a generally alkaline soil that is relatively low in nutrients but not impoverished. The second is a much richer and generally more moist and rather acidic soil. By adding organic matter and grit, you can amend or 'improve' your existing soil, but do remember that the organic matter should ideally be of animal manure rather than compost; almost by definition, meadows are grazed and animals mean manure.

After an appropriate soil, the second requirement is a reasonably high rainfall, and I wouldn't advise trying to develop an alpine meadow in a really dry part of the world.

Then establish the background planting. In the poorer type of alpine meadow, the 'background' plants will be grasses, but in a richer soil they should be much less important. The reason is that in a rich soil those plants, like the grasses, with a high demand for nitrogen will grow very rapidly and swamp the remainder. In the poorer soil, the grass should ideally be *Sesleria*,

The alpine greenhouse has no heat and is best thought of as a giant cloche

the moor grass, but this may be difficult to obtain and the next best bets would be some of the fescues. Avoid any of the species of *Poa* that are called meadow grasses because they have a very soft, lush foliage.

Within your overall background sowing of grasses, the other plants, the characteristic flowering species, must be established. I recommend strongly, however, that you do not try to do this directly from seed, for they will inevitably have difficulty competing with the grass, no matter how sparsely you have sown it. Obtain seed of the plants but sow it in a humus-enriched soil-based compost in pots in a cold frame, and plant out later.

In the richer, more moist soils, primulas must be your most important

The tall Himalayan poppy *Meconopsis betonicifolia* is suitable for borders or alpine meadows

plants and among those I would try hardest to establish are *Primula farinosa*, which is a native British species, *P. glutinosa*, from the Alps and a plant for the more acid soils, and the giant Himalayan cowslip, *P. florindae*.

You must have gentians, although you may be well advised to stick with those most readily raised from seed such as the willow gentian, *Gentiana asclepiadea*. My third big genus would, I think, be *Geranium*. Then, among the rather taller plants, persevere with *Meconopsis*, the blue Himalayan poppy, and some of the taller bulbous irises. There are many other species, too: *Hepatica nobilis*, crocuses, dwarf narcissi, some dwarf tulips, anemones and pulsatillas, *Corydalis* and alpine aster. Above everything, experiment.

An alpine meadow is a most challenging garden feature but, when done well, it can be magnificent

CARE AND MAINTENANCE

Alpines have many endearing features. Not least among them is that you have the option in your choice of species between those plants from unusual, specific and demanding environments that challenge all of your horticultural skills, and those many (including most plants recommended in this book) that require very little care but nonetheless will reward you amply.

The plants I describe here require less specific care, feeding and watering than those included in any other book in this series. They do not thrive on total neglect, however, and the following guidance should help you to obtain the best from them.

Planting

You will obtain most of your new stock as small plants in small containers from a garden centre or specialist

Terracotta pans provide an attractive and effective way to display an alpine collection

A mulch of stone chips sets off the beauty of alpine plants and protects their flowers from damage

nursery. They may be planted immediately and at any time of the year. For outdoor plantings, simply knock the plant in its ball of compost from the container and pull away the upper centimetre or so of compost which may contain moss, weeds or weed seeds. Then carefully pull away the surface grit from the planting position (don't contaminate it with soil), use a trowel to prepare a suitably sized hole, scatter bonemeal in the base, insert the plant and firm it in with your fingers. Then replace the surface layer of grit carefully around the plant. If the plants are to be kept in an alpine house, I strongly advise you to replace any plastic pot in which the plant is purchased with a terracotta one of similar size.

Feeding

I simply give each plant a light dusting with bonemeal early in the year. This contains phosphate to enhance root growth and a small amount of nitrogen for leaf and overall development. If plants are reluctant to flower, I use a very small dose of sulphate of potash. I don't give alpines any fertilizer that has a high nitrogen content as this encourages soft, lush growth that is prone to disease and other damage.

Watering

Other than in periods of prolonged dry weather, alpines in rock gardens, if they are correctly mulched with grit, should require no watering. Those in troughs or similar containers, like all container plants, will need additional watering in dry spells. Plants in alpine houses will, of course, require watering, but the gravel bed in which they are contained should maintain moisture reasonably well. Plants with very specific requirements of low pH should not be watered with hard (alkaline) tap water. Rain water should be used instead, but take care to filter water from rain-water butts which notoriously harbour pests, diseases and algal spores.

Protection

I've pointed out the advantages that an alpine greenhouse offers, but even plants that otherwise grow happily outdoors can suffer from the vagaries of the lowland winter. Most specifically, they may require protection to prevent damage to buds and flowers. In their native environment, seasons tend to be rather sharply marked. Once temperatures rise and the snow melts, winter weather does not return again. In our gardens, it often does at intervals through the early spring and tender flowers are then damaged. Small cloches, or even single sheets of glass, if well secured, provide very valuable protection at this time. It is also very important to check your plants regularly and remove any dead flowers, dead foliage or trapped leaves that have blown in from trees and shrubs nearby. These notoriously lodge among the cushions of alpines and serve as starting points for mould growth.

Weeding

Weed growth shouldn't be a problem in an established alpine bed, but it is worth taking two precautions. First, ensure that an outdoor rock garden is completely free of perennial weeds such as couch grass before you begin planting. It is extremely difficult to eradicate them later and this can really only be done by careful and regular application of a translocated weedkiller containing glyphosate. Also do take note of my suggestion to remove the top compost layer from the pots of newly purchased plants as this frequently harbours mosses, liverworts and, of course, weeds, especially the little hairy bitter cress which can so easily be introduced into your collection in this way.

Many species may need some form of cloche protection to guard against the clinging damp of a lowland winter

PROPAGATION

Most alpines are herbaceous perennials; many are true species, some are hybrids. A few are shrubs, a few are bulbs; only one of those I recommend here is an annual. All of this tells us something about propagating them.

Herbaceous perennials are most readily propagated by division or, if they are relatively large and bushy plants, from softwood or semi-ripe cuttings. All species should be capable of being propagated from seed, although rather commonly germination is slow and erratic. Hybrids and selected varieties generally do not come true from seed and must be divided. Shrubs are best propagated from semi-ripe cuttings taken in summer or from hardwood cuttings in late autumn or winter. Bulbs are best divided when dormant and, although some may be raised from seed, this is a slow process and flowering may take up to four years.

Seed

Seed should be as fresh as possible, although I realize that alpine seed is usually obtained from specialist suppliers or through society 'exchange' schemes and its freshness is therefore uncertain. It should be sown in a gritty soil-based compost of the type I recommend for plants. Generally it should be sown on the surface and then lightly covered with more compost, although a few types of alpine, most notably *Primula* species, should remain exposed. Place the seed pots or trays in a cold frame and leave them over winter. Germination should begin as temperatures rise in the spring, and the seedlings are then allowed to become well grown before being pricked out into individual pots, where they should remain for 12 months before being planted out.

Division

The age at which alpines should be divided depends on their rate of growth, but in most instances once the plant begins to intrude on its neighbours it is a good time to take action. The best times of year to divide are autumn or early spring (as the foliage dies down with bulbs) and the procedure is straightforward: use a small fork to dig up the mature clump and pull it first into two, then more, pieces. Discard those parts that were in the centre of the original crown and replant the remainder.

Cuttings

Softwood cuttings are taken early in the season, while the tissues are still soft and sappy. The ideal length for alpines is about 2cm (¾in) and they should always be handled carefully as the tissues, being soft, are readily damaged. Cuttings should be removed from the parent plant with a clean cut made

Cuttings offer a simple means of propagating the many types of alpine that don't come true from seed

close to a bud (if one is apparent). Moisten the freshly cut end of the cutting, dip it in fresh hormone rooting powder and then knock off the excess. Pipings are softwood cuttings taken from *Dianthus* species (pinks) where short lengths of stem tip are pulled away from the remainder, in a kind of telescope fashion.

Most plants produce semi-ripe cuttings during the second half of the summer and the best way of taking them from alpines is usually as a basal cutting, where a side-shoot is selected that is already 2–3cm (¾–1¼in) in length and then pulled or torn from its parent stem, to leave a small piece of the older stem at the base to form a 'heel'. Use hormone rooting powder as described above.

Softwood and semi-ripe cuttings should be rooted (or 'struck') in a covered propagator and placed in a cold frame. It's very important to maintain a moist atmosphere around the cuttings, for they will otherwise lose water through their leaves at a time when, lacking roots, they are unable to replace it from below. Even with a covered propagator, therefore, you should pay careful attention to the moisture content of the rooting medium and use a hand sprayer to mist over the cuttings regularly.

Hardwood cuttings are those taken of wood that has already become fairly tough, ideally during the current year. It's a mistake, though, to imagine that tough old wood from ancient branches can form hardwood cuttings. Timing is less critical for these cuttings and they can be taken at any time between autumn and winter. The shoot should be cut to a length of around 5cm (2in)

and inserted to about two-thirds of its length in a large pot in a cold frame. Hardwood cuttings of evergreens are more chancy, however, and the pot must be kept covered to minimize water loss through the leaves.

Layering

Some woody alpines root poorly from cuttings, but layering is a successful alternative. Select a low-growing shoot and strip off a section of leaves, starting about 5cm (2in) from the tip. Cut a shallow nick on the underside of the stem, pin the branch down into the soil and cover it with more soil. Leave the plant for about six months to develop roots. For the plants described in the Plant Directory, unless I have stated otherwise layering is best carried out in the autumn.

Alpine seeds are best left out during the winter in an open cold frame. Germination should begin when temperatures rise in spring

PESTS AND DISEASES

Most of the problems to which alpines are prone are those related to the climatic differences between the mountains and the lowlands. I have referred already to the damage that can ensure from frost damage to young flowers and the mould growth that develops around trapped leaves, for instance. Much of this can be prevented by careful attention to the routine techniques that I have outlined on pp. 14–15. Nonetheless, there are some specific pests and diseases that while not unique to alpines do commonly cause trouble on them, and the following chart should help you to identify and treat these. More information on plant problems can be found in my book *Best Garden Doctor*.

Vine weevils are the scourge of cyclamen, primulas and several other types of alpine

IDENTIFICATION OF COMMON PEST AND DISEASE PROBLEMS ON ALPINES

Symptom	Detail	Probable cause	Symptom	Detail	Probable cause
Symptoms on leaves			Mouldy	Grey, fluffy	Grey mould (*Botrytis*)
				White or pale grey	Mildew
Wilting	General	Short of water	Infested with insects	White, moth-like, tiny	Whiteflies
		Root pest or disease			
Holed	Generally ragged	Small pest (woodlice, millepedes)		Green, grey, black or other colour	Aphids
	Elongate holes, usually with slime present	Slugs or snails		Flat, like limpets	Scale insects
	Fairly large holes, over entire leaf or confined to edges	Caterpillars Beetles		Large, six legs (caterpillars)	Caterpillars
Discoloured	Mainly red	Short of water	Cobwebs present	Leaves usually bronzed or shrivelling	Red spider mite
	More or less bleached	Short of fertilizer Short of water Over-watered	**Symptoms on flowers**		
	Irregular yellowish patterns	Virus	Drooping	General	Short of water End of flowering period
	Irregular tunnels	Leaf miners	Tattered	Masses of tiny holes	Caterpillars
	Surface flecking	Leaf hoppers		Large pieces torn away (slime trails usually present)	Slugs or snails
	Brown (scorched)	Late frost in spring			
Spotted	Brown, irregular, no mould	Leaf spot		Large pieces torn away	Birds
	Small, dusty, black or yellow-orange	Rust	Discoloured	Powdery white covering	Mildew
			Mouldy	Fluffy grey mould	Grey mould (*Botrytis*)

TREATMENTS FOR COMMON PEST AND DISEASE PROBLEMS ON ALPINES

Problem	Recommended treatment
Aphids	Use a proprietary contact insecticide; pick off affected shoots by hand or wash off insects with the water jet from a hand sprayer. In an alpine house, use biological control.
Capsid bugs	Too erratic and unpredictable to make treatment feasible.
Caterpillars	Pick off by hand if the caterpillars can be found, but wear gloves as some people are allergic to their hairs. If masses of insects occur, pick off and destroy entire leaves, or use a contact insecticide or biological spray.
Fertilizer deficiency	Use a general balanced liquid fertilizer.
Grey mould	Pick off and destroy affected parts; spray with sulphur or a systemic fungicide.
Leaf hopper	Too erratic and unpredictable to make any treatment feasible.
Leaf miner	Remove and destroy affected leaves.
Leaf spot	In most instances, no treatment is necessary, but if symptoms appear to be related to overall poor growth replace affected plants.
Mildew	Apply sulphur or a systemic fungicide.
Red spider mites	No chemical treatment is feasible, but try not to allow plants to become too dry and hot. In an alpine house, use biological control.

Problem	Recommended treatment
Root disease	Destroy severely affected plants.
Root pests	For vine weevil, use biological control, which may have some effect on other root pests as well. Otherwise, remove and replace affected plants.
Rust	If a serious problem, spray plants with penconazole fungicide.
Scale insects	Pick off affected parts or spray plants with a systemic insecticide. In an alpine house, use biological control.
Slugs	Raise troughs on small 'feet' and ensure that a grit mulch is in place. This is normally successful, but if the problem persists apply slug pellets or biological control.
Snails	As for slugs (above).
Virus	Effects are usually mild so no treatment is necessary.
Whiteflies	No treatment is feasible on outdoor plants. In an alpine house, use biological control.
Woodlice	Dust plants with derris and try to locate and eradicate pests from their hiding places. Raising troughs on small 'feet' will help to discourage woodlice from accumulating underneath.

SOME FUNGICIDES, PESTICIDES AND BIOLOGICAL CONTROLS USEFUL FOR COMBATING PROBLEMS ON ALPINES

Fungicides	Uses and comments
Carbendazim	Systemic*, for most foliage and stem diseases, including the two important diseases grey mould and mildew
Myclobutanil	Systemic, especially useful for leaf spots and rust
Penconazole	Systemic, especially useful for leaf spots and rust
Triforine	Systemic, many foliage diseases
Sulphur**	Non-systemic, many foliage diseases

Insecticides	Uses and comments
Butoxycarboxim	Systemic on impregnated card 'pins', sap-sucking pests
Derris**	Contact, most pests
Natural soaps**	Contact, most pests
Permethrin	Contact, most pests
Pirimicarb	Contact, specific to aphids
Pyrethrum**	Contact, most pests

Slug and snail killers	Uses and comments
Methiocarb	As pellets
Metaldehyde	As pellets, mini-pellets or liquid

Biological controls**	Uses and comments
Steinernema carpocapsae	Nematode to control vine weevil (outdoors and alpine house)
Heterorhabditis megidis	Nematode to control vine weevil (outdoors and alpine house)
Phasmarhabditis hermaphroditica	Nematode to control slugs (outdoors)
Phytoseiulus persimilis	Predatory mite to control red spider mite (alpine house)
Encarsia formosa	Parasitic wasp to control whitefly (alpine house)
Aphidius matricariae	Parasitic wasp to control aphids (alpine house)
Metaphycus helvolus	Parasitic wasp to control scale insects (alpine house)
Bacillus thuringiensis	Bacterial spray to control caterpillars (outdoors and alpine house)

* Systemic substances are absorbed by the plant and require less frequent and less accurate spraying than contact materials

** Generally acceptable to organic gardeners

NB it should be noted that some of the chemicals mentioned are only available in particular formulations or in combination with certain other chemicals. Some may also be marketed for specific pest or disease problems only. In every case, you *must read the label directions carefully* to be sure that the product is being used for the purpose and in the manner for which it is intended. The names given in the table are those of the active ingredients. These will usually be different from the product or brand name but will be found printed on the label.

Acaena
New Zealand burr

"*I have long admired acaenas but soon realized that they are definitely subjects for the larger alpine planting. Even in my own garden, they are fairly invasive, but it was only when I had seen them growing in their native New Zealand that I fully realized what they are capable of achieving. So take my advice: grow them and admire them, but don't plant them close to anything small and innocent.*"

Origin New Zealand.
Habit Creeping evergreen, making a dense mat of foliage.
Flowering Season Summer, but flowers insignificant.
Size 2.5–5 x 15–75cm (1–2 x 6–30in).
Site Full sun or partial shade and well-drained soil. Ideal for poor or sandy sites.
Best Grown Outdoors, between paving (although less satisfactory where walked on) or in a large rock garden.

Features Small leaves in interesting colours, including a blue-grey that is very close to real blue, with curiously attractive and also very colourful spiky fruits (burrs).
Special Care None.
Propagation Lift and divide plants in spring, or replant self-rooting stolons. May also be raised from seed sown in autumn or early spring.
Problems Vigorous plants that may be invasive.

Acaena microphylla

Recommended Varieties
Acaena buchananii low, dense mat of grey-green foliage bearing yellow-brown burrs in late summer, 2.5 x 75cm (1 x 30in); *A. microphylla* AGM popular species with leaves that age from silver-grey to bronze and eye-catching burrs of bright crimson in mid- to late summer, 5 x 15cm (2 x 6in), 'Kupferteppich' (syn. *A.* 'Copper Carpet', *A.* 'Purple Carpet') is more vigorous, spreading to 60cm (24in), but has very striking copper-black foliage.

Achillea Yarrow

"*There are a number of plant genera that find their way into ornamental plant descriptions even though most gardeners spend a good deal of time trying to eradicate them. Yarrow is one, a common enough lawn weed as its native species* Achillea millefolium *but with some very pretty European relatives.*"

Origin Europe, alpine species mostly from Greece or the eastern Alps.
Habit Herbaceous perennials, most with a creeping, mat-like habit.
Flowering Season Mostly summer.
Size 15–30 x 25–40cm (6–12 x 10–16in).
Site Full sun, and a good choice for dry or poor soils.
Best Grown Outdoors, in a rock garden or between paving.

Recommended Varieties
Achillea ageratifolia AGM evergreen with tufts of spoon-shaped, grey-white leaves that form basal rosettes, solitary heads of white flowers in mid- to late summer, central Balkans, 20 x 30cm (8 x 12in); *A. chrysocoma* (syn. *A. aurea*) highly aromatic, woolly, grey-green foliage forms an evergreen mat with bright yellow flowers in early to midsummer, Albania and Macedonia, 20 x 40cm (8 x 16in); *A. clavennae* (syn. *A. argentea*) prostrate stems give this semi-evergreen species a mat-like habit, while white, hairy foliage and white daisy flowers in mid- to late summer make it an attractive plant but it is intolerant of winter wet, eastern Alps and western Balkans, 15 x 25cm (6 x 10in); *A. tomentosa* AGM widely available plant with soft, feathery clumps of grey-silver ever-green foliage and dense clusters of yellow flowerheads in late spring to early summer, south-west Europe to central Italy, 30 x 40cm (12 x 16in).

Features Tiny flowers in dense heads, some almost flat; highly attractive to insects and, in many species, lasting well into late summer. Most have pretty, feathery, aromatic foliage.
Special Care None.
Propagation Lift and divide plants in autumn or spring. Take semi-ripe cuttings in early summer.
Problems None.

Adonis Pheasant's eye

> *After snowdrops, I think that the first appearance of golden aconites is my favourite gardening event of the new season. And if you like aconites, you will surely love this bolder, grander version.*

Adonis amurensis 'Flore Pleno'

Origin Japan.
Habit Clump-forming herbaceous perennials.
Flowering Season Late winter to early spring.
Size 30 x 23cm (12 x 9in).
Site Partial shade and acidic soil or one enriched with leaf mould.
Best Grown Outdoors, in a rock garden or border.

Features Attractive combination of foliage and very vivid early flowers.
Special Care None.
Propagation Lift and divide plants after flowering, remove self-sown seedlings or sow seed in late summer.
Problems None.

Recommended Varieties
Adonis amurensis bold, golden-yellow flowers, like a large winter aconite, often bronzed on the outside, with clumps of finely divided, feathery leaves, 'Flore Pleno' is a double-flowered form.

Alchemilla Lady's mantle

> *Alchemilla is another of those much loved garden plant genera where the more familiar border version of* Alchemilla mollis *has a neater, smaller but no less attractive alpine relative. Imagine a version scaled down in all its parts, and scaled down in its ground-covering capabilities, and you will envisage* Alchemilla alpina.

Origin Europe.
Habit Low, mound- or clump-forming herbaceous perennials.
Flowering Season Summer.
Size 15–20 x 20–45cm (6–8 x 8–18in).
Site Sun or shade and all soils except waterlogged.
Best Grown Outdoors, in a rock garden or at the front of a border.

Features Easy to grow, forming low mounds of green foliage with lobed or rounded leaves and masses of tiny yellow-green flowers.
Special Care None.
Propagation Lift and divide plants in autumn or spring, or sow seed in spring or autumn.
Problems None, but will self-seed.

Recommended Varieties
Alchemilla alpina (alpine lady's mantle) superficially very much like a miniature form of the more familiar *A. mollis* but with differences in the leaves, *A. alpina* having dark green leaves with deep lobes, smooth above and with hairy undersides. They still have, however, that endearing feature of trapping small drops of water like beads of mercury. Typical *Alchemilla* flowers are held in upright clusters, mountains throughout much of Europe, 15 x 45cm (6 x 18in); *A. erythropoda* AGM clump-forming plant with hairy, blue-green leaves that have shallow lobes and typical lady's mantle flowers, western Carpathians and Balkan mountains, 20 x 20cm (8 x 8in).

PERENNIALS AND SHRUBS

Anacyclus

❝ *There are many alpine daisies, almost all producing admiration and delight in equal measure. This one always seems to produce surprise, too, because for some unaccountable reason it doesn't seem to be very widely known, something that I hope this recommendation will put right. If it has a drawback over some of the other alpine daisies, it is that it seems unusually prone to damage from winter wet.* ❞

Origin Morocco.
Habit Low-growing evergreen mat.
Flowering Season Late spring to late summer.
Size 5 x 25cm (2 x 10in).
Site Sheltered, sunny position and very well-drained soil.
Best Grown Outdoors, in a rock garden, or in an alpine house.

Features Finely divided grey-green leaves and daisy-like flowers.
Special Care Dead-head to prolong flowering. Protect from wet winter weather with a gravel mulch and a cloche.
Propagation Sow seed in spring or take softwood cuttings in summer.
Problems Aphids, slugs.

Recommended Varieties
Anacyclus pyrethrum var. *depressus* a form of the Atlas Mountain daisy with white flowers with crimson undersides.

Anagallis Pimpernel

❝ *The connection between the plant and the fictional hero is that the individual flowers, too, appear fleetingly. There is also a floral red pimpernel but this is its electric-blue southern European relative.* ❞

Features Mounds of branching stems and striking flowers.
Special Care A short-lived perennial that is usually treated as an annual.
Propagation Take semi-ripe cuttings in summer or sow ripe seed in autumn.
Problems Aphids, slugs.

Origin South-west Europe.
Habit Spreading evergreens.
Flowering Season Late spring to autumn.
Size 15 x 40cm (6 x 16in).
Site Sunny position and well-drained soil; intolerant of winter wet.
Best Grown Outdoors in a rock garden or front of a border.

Recommended Varieties
Anagallis monellii AGM deep blue, saucer-shaped flowers, often with a red eye.

Androsace Rock jasmine

❝ *I find that alpine enthusiasts who adore primulas tend to be less enthusiastic about their close relatives in the genus* Androsace*; by contrast,* Androsace *devotees tend not to collect primulas. I confess that I come into the former category and find the flower colours of* Androsace *less endearing as they are less subtle; but the plants still sell in their hundreds.* ❞

Origin *Androsace carnea* Alps and Pyrenees, *A. sarmentosa* Kumaon to western China, *A. sempervivoides* western Himalayas.
Habit Mostly cushion- or mat-forming evergreens.
Flowering Season Mostly mid- to late spring.
Size Most 8–10 x 20–30cm (3–4 x 8–12in).
Size Sunny position and well-drained soil that must not dry out in summer.
Best Grown Outdoors, in a rock garden, trough, raised bed or wall crevice, or in an alpine house.

Androsace carnea

Features Most form cushions of tight leaf rosettes or loose mats of evergreen foliage, with brightly coloured flowers.

Special Care Plants grown outside may need protection overhead from winter wet and from rotting around the crown (use a gravel mulch). Plants grown in pots in an alpine house must be kept moist at the roots in the summer.

Propagation Sow ripe seed in late

Recommended Varieties
Androsace carnea (pink rock jasmine) a very popular plant with a dense rosette of green grass-like leaves topped with clusters of pink flowers in summer, subsp. *brigantiaca* larger rosettes and white flowers on 15cm (6in) stalks, subsp. *laggeri* AGM small rosettes, very narrow leaves and deep magenta-pink flowers, subsp. *rosea* (syn. var. *halleri*) AGM more vigorous with larger rosettes and more open pink flowers, easy to grow and self-seeds freely; *A. sarmentosa* (syn. *A. primuloides*) AGM one of the larger species, forming a loose mat that spreads by red runners, the woolly leaf rosette bears large flowers of bright pink to mauve-red on 5–10cm (2–4in) stalks, from late spring to early summer, 'Chumbyi' is more hairy and forms a dense mat, 'Sherriff's' has silver foliage and pale pink flowers; *A. sempervivoides* (syn. *A. mucronifolia*) AGM easy-to-grow mat-like plant that spreads by short red runners, with flat rosettes of leathery, deep green leaves and clusters of bright pink flowers on 8cm (3in) stems.

summer or autumn, lift and divide plants in autumn or take softwood cuttings in summer.
Problems Aphids, slugs.

Anemone Wind flower

❝ Anemone *is a big genus, ranging from invasive border perennials through the brightly coloured St Brigid and De Caen cut-flower varieties to the tiny, delicate bulbous plants that I recommend here. But delicate and tiny though they may be, some will spread with abandon, so do give them space to produce the carpet of flowers that displays them at their best.* ❞

Features Very good plants to spread naturally, given space; striking spring flowers that look far more delicate than they really are.

Anemone blanda 'White Charmer'

Special Care None.
Propagation Lift and divide plants after flowering or sow ripe seed in late summer.
Problems None.

Origin Europe.
Habit Mostly leafy, clump-forming plants, some rhizomatous, others tuberous.
Flowering Season Early to mid-spring.
Size 15–20 x 30cm (6–8 x 12in).
Site Varies greatly (see below).
Best Grown Outdoors, in a rock garden.

Recommended Varieties
Anemone apennina (blue wood anemone) AGM woodland plant for a cool, partially shaded rock garden, with bright blue, star-like flowers in early spring; *A. blanda* tuberous species for a hot, dry position or a pot, although more shade tolerant than often suggested, star-like flowers in blue, purple, pink or white in early to mid-spring, may be invasive, 'blue' (an informal name used for a range of very good forms) mid-blue flowers, 'Radar' AGM deep magenta flowers with a white centre, 'White Splendour' AGM large white flowers; *A. nemorosa* (wood anemone) woodland plant for sun or partial shade, with white cup-shaped flowers often flushed with pink, best named varieties are 'Alba Plena' double white flowers, 'Allenii' AGM large lavender-blue flowers, 'Robinsoniana' AGM pale lavender-blue flowers with grey reverse.

PERENNIALS AND SHRUBS

Antennaria Everlasting

❝ *Many of the best alpine members of the daisy family don't have the typical daisy flowers of a central disc surrounded by rays, and this is another. The flowers are tufted like tiny paint brushes, surrounded by papery bracts. I find it blends particularly well with* Armeria. ❞

Origin Throughout Europe, especially in mountainous areas, also northern Asia and North America.
Habit Spreading, evergreen or semi-evergreen mats of creeping stems.
Flowering Season Late spring to early summer.
Size 10 x 60cm (4 x 24in).
Site Full sun and well-drained soil.
Best Grown Outdoors, but too invasive for troughs.

Features Silver foliage and small clusters of white or pink flowers with no ray florets.
Special Care None.
Propagation Lift and divide plants in spring or replant rooted runners. Sow ripe seed in autumn or early winter.
Problems None.

Recommended Varieties
Antennaria dioica (syn. *Gnaphalium dioicum, Omalotheca dioica*) (catsfoot) neat silver-white, woolly leaves and white to pink-brown bracts, 'Nyewoods Variety' good compact form with rose-pink flowers.

Aquilegia Columbine

❝ *I hesitated before including* Aquilegia *in the book. Although there's no doubt that they grow in the high mountains, and* Aquilegia alpina *has a name to prove it, they are plants of the alpine meadow and the plants have a height to match.* ❞

Origin Europe, Japan.
Habit Basal clumps of herbaceous foliage and slender flowering stems.
Flowering Season Mid-spring to summer.
Size Varies, *A. alpina* 45–60 x 30cm (18–24 x 12in) but others mostly 25 x 25cm (10 x 10in).
Site Full sun and gritty, well-drained soil.
Best Grown Outdoors, the taller ones in a border, others in a rock garden or scree.

Features Lacy foliage and nodding flowers, often with spurs. Even the taller species have stems stiff enough to require no staking; a short flowering season is the only real drawback with these plants.

Arabis Rock cress

❝ *Some years ago, when I was looking over a cottage garden on behalf of a prospective purchaser to see what potential it offered, I came face to face instead with the potential of* Arabis alpina. *A previous owner (probably not all that many years previously) had planted it to grow on and tumble from a low front wall. Sadly, it had tumbled rather too much and not only had the low wall totally disappeared, but so had a large part of the front garden. Be warned.* ❞

Recommended Varieties
Aquilegia alpina (alpine columbine) bright blue nodding flowers with spurs set off by grey-green foliage, often seen naturally in a damp rock crevice, although it grows rather tall for an alpine and is a classic plant for an alpine meadow; *A. bertolonii* AGM dainty species from south-eastern France and northern Italy that is only 15cm (6in) high, leaves are dark green and flowers violet-blue with incurved spurs and downward-turned sepals; *A. flabellata* AGM Japanese species with blue-green leaves and sturdy blue-mauve flowers tipped with white, flowers have short hooked spurs, var. *pumila* (syn. 'Nana') AGM most commonly grown form, a dwarf only 10–20cm (4–8in) high.

Special Care None.
Propagation Seed is readily produced but hybridizes with neighbouring plants such as *A. vulgaris*. Lift and divide plants in spring, although older individuals will prove difficult to divide successfully because they will have developed a robust tap-root.
Problems Leaf miners, aphids, mildew.

Origin Mostly eastern Europe, south-west Asia.
Habit Evergreen mat-forming perennials.
Flowering Season Spring or summer.
Size 20–25 x 45–60cm (8–10 x 18–24in).
Site Most prefer a sunny site, tolerating hot, dry conditions and poor soils, but A. alpina and A. ferdinandi-coburgi 'Old Gold' also tolerate partial shade.
Best Grown Outdoors; use as a path edging or grow over a dry wall or bank.

Arabis alpina 'Flore Pleno'

Features Dense mats of foliage with clusters of small flowers.
Special Care Trim lightly after flowering to encourage a bushy habit.
Propagation Take softwood cuttings in summer, or lift and divide established plants after flowering. Species come true from seed sown in spring or autumn.
Problems Aphids, caterpillars, downy mildew, white blister, arabis midge.

Recommended Varieties
Arabis alpina subsp. *caucasica* (syn. A. albida, A. caucasica), a spreading mat suitable for edging a path or to drape over a dry wall – however it is invasive. 'Flore Pleno' has double white flowers, 'Variegata' has a white edge to the leaves; A. blepharophylla rather short lived, rosettes of grey-green leaves with flowers that vary from white to deep pink; A. ferdinandi-coburgi 'Old Gold' somewhat atypical-looking arabis, the main feature being flat rosettes of fleshy leaves covered with green and gold variegations, although it also has white flowers.

Arenaria Sandwort

❝ *A plant called sandwort might be thought to be something from the seashore. While it's true that some seashore plants, paradoxically, also live in mountains and make good alpine subjects, this is not one of them. Arenaria is paradoxical in some other ways, too, because, while its name refers to its need for a sandy, well-drained soil, it does also, and unlike many alpines, need a moist environment to thrive.* ❞

Features Dainty, almost star-like flowers.
Special Care None.
Propagation Sow seed in autumn or early spring. Lift and divide A. balearica and A. montana after flowering. Take semi-ripe cuttings of A. purpurascens in spring or summer.

Problems Some may be weedy and invasive, but of those recommended below only A. balearica shows this tendency.

Origin A. balearica Balearic Islands, Corsica, Sardinia and other western Mediterranean islands, A. montana Spain, Portugal and western France, A. purpurascens damp rocky places in the Pyrenees.
Habit Loose mats or cushions; those recommended below are evergreen.
Flowering Season Late spring to early summer.
Size 3–10 x 20–50cm (1¼–4 x 8–20in).
Site A. balearica requires partial shade, A. montana is best in sun, A. purpurascens thrives in either. Soil should be well drained and fairly poor.
Best Grown Outdoors, in a rock garden or trough.

Recommended Varieties
Arenaria balearica (mossy sandwort) spreading green mat up to 50cm (20in) wide, small white flowers on slender stalks, ideal for growing over damp rocks; A. montana AGM sprawling perennial that forms a loose mat of hairy, grey-green foliage ideal for cascading over a crevice, rather showy white flowers are borne on 10–20cm (4–8in) stems; A. purpurascens (pink sandwort) summer-flowering species, one of the prettiest with small clusters of pink, purple or white flowers and loose cushions of pointed leaves.

PERENNIALS AND SHRUBS

Armeria Thrift, Sea pink

❝ *Readers old enough to remember the 12-sided British nickel-brass threepenny piece (it was discontinued in 1971) may remember the emblem on its reverse side. It was a picture of* Armeria maritima, *the sea thrift, the idea being a play on words in that the threepenny piece was intended to find its way into the money boxes of the thrifty and so encourage saving. I hope that the plant itself finds its way into everyone's rock garden – although you will have to pay more than three pence to buy one now.* ❞

Origin A. juniperifolia Spain, A. maritima most of Europe, especially on sea cliffs.
Habit Compact evergreen cushions.
Flowering Season Late spring to early summer.
Size 20–25 x 25–50cm (8–10 x 10–20in).
Site Full sun and light, free-draining, fairly poor soil.
Best Grown Outdoors, in a rock garden or large trough; A. juniperifolia is neat enough for a smaller trough.

Recommended Varieties
Armeria juniperifolia (syn. A. caespitosa) AGM neat tuft of grey-green foliage with lilac-pink flowers on short stems, 'Bevan's Variety' AGM has a dense cushion of foliage and deep rose-pink flowers; A. maritima (syn. A. vulgaris; common thrift) variable in habit and flower colour, to be more certain of colour and a neater plant choose var. *alba* large white flowers on short stalks, 'Düsseldorfer Stolz' (syn. 'A. D. Pride') rich crimson flowers, or 'Laucheana' deep pink.

Armeria maritima 'Alba'

Features Tufts of grassy foliage and globular flowers.
Special Care None.
Propagation Lift and divide plants after flowering. Species may be raised from seed sown in autumn or early winter.
Problems None.

Artemisia

❝ *There are a great many artemisias. Most are weedy things, and even those that find their way into herb gardens certainly don't do so because of the beauty of their flowers. However, most do have rather attractive filigree, feathery foliage and, when this is combined with a dwarf habit, a few rock garden subjects materialize. But remember that the foliage is also woolly and attracts clinging moisture.* ❞

Origin A. caucasica limestone rocks of southern and central Europe; A. schmidtiana Japan.
Habit Neat sub-shrubs.
Flowering Season Summer.
Size 5–10 x 15–30cm (2–4 x 6–12in).
Site Full sun and light, fertile soil.
Best Grown Outdoors, in a rock garden or large trough.

Features Grown for their silver-grey foliage rather than their flowers.
Special Care None.
Propagation Lift and divide plants in spring or take softwood cuttings in early summer.
Problems Aphids, rust.

Asperula Woodruff

❝ *The family Rubiaceae is a huge one, mainly from warm climates so you wouldn't expect it to include many alpines. There are a few nonetheless, all with the same tiny tubular flowers that characterize the group; and if you think they look familiar, their close relatives include such familiar wild flowers as the bedstraws and goose grass.* ❞

Origin *A. gussonii* northern Sicily; *A. lilaciflora* subsp. *lilaciflora* eastern Mediterranean; *A. suberosa* mountains of Greece and Bulgaria.
Habit Cushion-forming; all those recommended below are evergreen.
Flowering Season Early summer.
Size 2.5–5 x 30cm (1–2 x 12in).
Site Sun, but intolerant of very high temperatures; soil should be free draining.
Best Grown Alpine house, apart from *A. gussonii* which may be grown in a scree garden or planted in tufa.

Features Cushions of weak stems and stalkless tubular flowers.
Special Care *A. suberosa* has a tendency to die back; affected stems should be removed promptly.
Propagation Take semi-ripe cuttings in mid-spring.
Problems Aphids, slugs, and grey mould in winter.

Recommended Varieties

Asperula gussonii tuft of slender stems arising from a woody base, foliage dark green and flowers flesh-pink; *A. lilaciflora* subsp. *lilaciflora* foliage is heath-like and forms a cushion that is sometimes prostrate, flowers are rich pink, may be grown either as a pan plant in an alpine house or in a trough; *A. suberosa* best grown in an alpine house in a pan, where its frail stems may be protected and its need for a very well-drained soil met, the heath-like leaves are covered in white wool and form a 8cm (3in) high cushion, in early summer there is a cluster of soft pink flowers.

Aster alpinus

Aster

❝ *I think most gardeners probably realize that their garden asters aren't* Aster *while their Michaelmas daisies are. The garden aster, so good for cutting, is* Callistephus. *But the plants here are dwarf alpine Michaelmas daisies.* ❞

Origin *A. alpinus* mountains of Europe and Asia in dry meadows and rocky places, *A. natalensis* South Africa.
Habit Rosettes or mats; all those recommended below are herbaceous.
Flowering Season Summer.
Size 10–25 x 25cm (4–10 x 10in).
Site Full sun and reasonably fertile, free-draining soil.
Best Grown Outdoors, in a rock garden.

Features *A. alpinus* has a neat basal rosette of spoon-shaped leaves; *A. natalensis* has a mat-like habit.
Special Care None.
Propagation Lift and divide plants in spring, or sow ripe seed in autumn.
Problems None.

Recommended Varieties

Aster alpinus (alpine aster) AGM neat plant but the species does vary in size and flower colour (violet, white or pink), so either buy in flower or seek out named varieties; *A. natalensis* (syn. *Felicia rosulata*) dense mat of rich green, spoon-shaped leaves, with fine deep blue flowers borne on 10–15cm (4–6in) stems.

PERENNIALS AND SHRUBS

Astilbe

❝ *People ask me rather often if there are plants that I can't stand. Forced to respond, there's a good chance that astilbes might be among my answers. So what are they doing here? Largely, my dislike extends to the border perennials, many of which have colours that verge on the luminous and that I find repellent. The alpine forms are scaled-down versions but they do have more charm, and so I scale down my dislike in proportion.* ❞

Features Fern-like leaves and feathery flower spikes.
Special Care None.
Propagation Lift and divide plants in spring. Seed germination is slow and named varieties will not come true.
Problems Powdery mildew. May be invasive.

Origin *A. chinensis* var. *pumila* China, *A. glaberrima* var. *saxatilis* and *A. simplicifolia* Japan.
Habit Clump-forming herbaceous perennials.
Flowering Season Mid- to late summer.
Size 23 x 23cm (9 x 9in), except *A. chinensis* var. *pumila* 30 x 40cm (12 x 16in).
Site Partial shade and moist, moderately fertile soil.
Best Grown Outdoors; ideal rock plants to grow near to water.

Recommended Varieties
Astilbe chinensis var. *pumila* AGM more compact form of the species with dense spikes of rose-mauve flowers; *A. glaberrima* var. *saxatilis* AGM best variety of this species with bronze fern-like foliage and pink flowers; *A. simplicifolia* AGM deeply cut fern-like foliage and spikes of white or pale pink flowers, buy a named variety if you want a specific flower colour.

Astilbe chinensis var. pumila

Aubrieta

❝ *Named after the great French botanical artist Claude Aubriet but known to everyone not as aubrieta but as aubretia, this plant is among the most familiar and welcome signs of spring. Plant a blend of differently coloured varieties close together and the effect is splendid – and it's not often I say that about mixed varieties. But do be sure to include some double-flowered forms.* ❞

Astragalus Milk vetch

❝ *No gardening books seem to mention* Astragalus, *and I don't know why. Admittedly, many of the species have a reputation merely as wayside weeds, but this is, after all, the largest genus in the entire pea family with around 2,000 species, so it's a shame that gardeners can't find room for one or two.* ❞

Origin North America.
Habit Prostrate semi-evergreen bush.
Flowering Season Summer.
Size 15 x 60cm (6 x 24in).
Site Full sun and light, sandy soil.
Best Grown Outdoors, in a rock garden or trough.

Features Pea-like flowers.
Special Care None.
Propagation Sow seed in autumn or take semi-ripe cuttings in summer.
Problems Intolerant of root disturbance.

Recommended Varieties
Astragalus utahensis (syn. *A. halleri*) purple flowers.

Features Grey-green foliage with clusters of four-petalled, cross-shaped flowers covering the plant.
Special Care Trim back after flowering to keep compact.
Propagation Increase named forms from softwood cuttings taken in summer.
Problems Downy and powdery mildew, which can seriously disfigure the plants after flowering when they should be cut back.

Origin Dry rocky places in mountains of south-eastern Europe.
Habit Spreading evergreen mats.
Flowering Season Spring.
Size 15 x 60cm (6 x 24in).
Site Full sun, thriving in neutral or chalky soils. Ideal coastal plant.
Best Grown Outdoors; very commonly grown (and very effective) tumbling over a rocky wall. Also ideal for crevices or growing on its side in a rock garden, and good between paving (but not to be walked on) or on a sunny slope.

Recommended Varieties
There are many named varieties, mostly derived from *Aubrieta deltoidea*; the following are a personal selection of those that I have grown: 'Astolat' single, purple flowers and variegated foliage, 'Aureovariegata' single, pale lavender-blue flowers and yellow-variegated leaves, 'Doctor Mules' AGM old variety with rich violet-blue flowers, 'Greencourt Purple semi-double, dark purple flowers, 'Red Carpet' single, deep red, flowers.

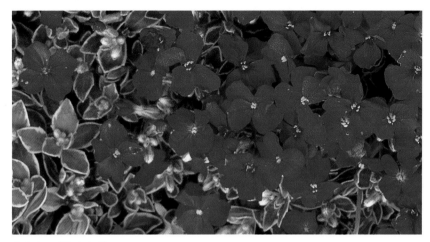

Aubrieta 'Astolat'

Aurinia Golden alyssum, Gold dust

❝ It's alphabetical coincidence that brings together two plants that are often brought together in the garden. But, like aubrieta, this too is a plant that has a name which isn't all it seems. For Aurinia *is the golden alyssum so beloved of generations of cottage gardeners. ❞*

Origin Rocky highlands of central and south-eastern Europe.
Habit Evergreen sub-shrub forming a low, loose hummock.
Flowering Season Mid-spring to early summer.
Size 30 x 50cm (12 x 20in).
Site Sunny, sheltered site and well-drained soil.
Best Grown Outdoors, in a large rockery, scree, raised bed or on a bank.

Features One of the easiest alpines to grow. Masses of tiny ochre-yellow flowers in such profusion as to conceal the leaves.
Special Care Cut back woody stems lightly after flowering in order to keep the plant neat and compact.
Propagation Sow seed of the species in winter or early spring. Take semi-ripe cuttings of named varieties in summer.
Problems None, but does self-seed, although seldom really aggressively.

Recommended Varieties
Aurinia saxatilis (syn. *Alyssum saxatile*) AGM a mass of bright yellow flowers arising from among the oval, silver-grey leaves, 'Compactum' (syn. 'Compacta') as its name suggests, a compact dwarf form only 10cm (4in) high, 'Dudley Nevill' unusual buff-yellow flowers, 'Variegata' leaves with creamy white margins, 'Flore Pleno' double yellow flowers.

PERENNIALS AND SHRUBS

Calceolaria Slipper flower

❝ At the risk of being boring, I will say that this is yet another plant (see Astilbe *on p. 28) that really is so ungainly and unattractive in its more familiar large-flowered form as a pot plant and yet so endearing and dainty in its small, alpine form. But I suppose the contrast is no more unusual than the fact that pretty little lambs grow into sheep. ❞*

Features Neat basal rosette of hairy, oval leaves. The main attraction is the unusual pouch-shaped flowers.

Special Care Soil must be kept moist.

Propagation Lift and divide plants in spring, or sow seed in a cold frame in autumn or early spring.

Problems Aphids, slugs, grey mould.

> **Origin** Chile.
> **Habit** Evergreen rosettes.
> **Flowering Season** Summer.
> **Size** 25 x 20cm (10 x 8in).
> **Site** Partial shade and cool, humus-rich soil.
> **Best Grown** Outdoors, in a rock garden or large trough.

> **Recommended Varieties**
> *Calceolaria biflora* (syn. *C. plantaginea*) hardy species with clusters of small yellow flowers, each 2.5cm (1in) across.

Calluna Heather, Ling

❝ Heather, certainly in its normal wild form, isn't a plant for a small rock garden, nor for any garden than doesn't have an acidic soil. But, in one or other of its selected varieties, it really can be a very important part of larger, wilder rock gardens – perhaps those created at the edge of the moors that are its natural habitat. ❞

> **Origin** *C. vulgaris* native to most of north and west Europe, northern Asia and western North America, often blanketing extensive heaths and moorland.
> **Habit** Dwarf evergreen shrub.
> **Flowering Season** Summer.
> **Size** Varies, but low-growing forms for rock gardens are 10–25 x 30–50cm (4–10 x 12–20in).
> **Site** Best in full sun but tolerates light shade. Soil must be acidic and free draining; will not survive on alkaline or waterlogged soils. Where garden soil is unsuitable, small varieties may be grown in troughs or other containers of lime-free compost. Excellent for a windy, exposed garden or a sunny slope.
> **Best Grown** Outdoors, in a rock garden.

Features Tiny, scale-like leaves give the plants a feathery appearance; the leaf colour, especially on cultivated forms, changes through the seasons. Masses of small flowers are produced in shades of mauve, red, pink or white.

Special Care When mulching, use an acidic material such as chopped conifer needles. Feed in spring with rose fertilizer. Regular clipping is worthwhile as the plants soon become unkempt if neglected; use single-handed shears after flowering or in early spring.

Propagation Take short semi-ripe cuttings in early summer, or layer in late summer.

Problems Roots may rot in wet soils and stems can die back.

Calluna vulgaris 'Spring Cream'

Recommended Varieties

Calluna vulgaris is very variable and rarely grown as the true species. There are several hundred named varieties, but the following are both reliable and compact unless stated otherwise: 'County Wicklow' AGM double pink flowers, 'Kinlochruel' AGM double white flowers, 'Robert Chapman' AGM golden leaves in spring, changing through orange and bronze to red in winter, purple flowers, vigorous tall bush, 'Sir John Charrington' AGM yellow-gold leaves, turning orange with red shoot tips in winter, dark red flowers, compact and bushy, 'Sunset' AGM gold-yellow leaves in spring, turning orange in summer, red-bronze in winter, mauve-pink flowers.

Campanula
Bellflower, harebell

❝ *The Blue Bell of Scotland'* (not, as it's often called, the 'Bluebells') must be one of the best-loved British folk songs. It sprang up mysteriously at the end of the eighteenth century. Its inspiration had been springing up for many centuries before that, however, but it isn't Hyacinthoides non-scripta, the bluebell of English woods, but a species of Campanula, known south of the border as the harebell. And there are several dainty little members of this large and attractive genus that should spring up in your rock garden. ❞

Origin *C. carpatica* Carpathian Mountains, *C. cochleariifolia* mountains of central and southern Europe such as the Alps and Pyrenees, *C. elatines* north-west Italy, *C. garganica* southern Italy and Cephalonia.

Habit Herbaceous, with a spreading tuft or mat of stems.

Flowering Season Summer, some into the autumn.

Size 5–15 x 30–60cm (2–6 x 12–24in).

Site Sunny position generally best but *C. cochleariifolia* and *C. garganica* will tolerate partial shade. Soil should be well drained but retain moisture during summer.

Best Grown Outdoors; generally a little too vigorous for troughs.

Campanula carpatica **'Weisse Clips'**

Features Easy-to-grow plants that add colour to rock gardens in summer when many other alpines have finished flowering. Some are only suitable for larger rock gardens. The leaves are oval and toothed and the flowers cup shaped or characteristic nodding bells.

Special Care None.

Propagation Lift and divide plants after flowering. Raise from seed sown in autumn or late winter, or take softwood cuttings in summer.

Problems *C. carpatica* and *C. garganica* can self-seed and become invasive.

Recommended Varieties

Campanula carpatica AGM popular rock plant, the bright green tuft of leaves and large purple-blue flowers look effective but it can swamp neighbours, good named varieties include 'Blaue Clips' (syn. 'Blue Clips') very large, sky-blue flowers, and 'Weisse Clips' (syn. 'White Clips') pure white flowers, both come true from seed; *C. cochleariifolia* (syn. *C. pusilla*) AGM charming plant only 10cm (4in) high with pale blue bells, suitable for a wall crevice, scree or large trough, most named varieties have varying shades of blue flowers but var. *alba* is white; *C. elatines* smaller version of *C. garganica* (below) that may be grown outdoors or in a pan in an alpine house; *C. garganica* AGM almost evergreen, forming clumps 5 x 30cm (2 x 12in), bright green heart-shaped leaves contrast with the star-like, pale lavender flowers which continue well into autumn, easy to grow and a good subject for planting in a wall crevice or for overhanging rocks.

PERENNIALS AND SHRUBS

Cassiope

" Cassiope has a classical pedigree; she was the wife of Cepheus, King of Ethiopia, and the mother of Andromeda. In botanical reality, however, Cassiope is a cousin of Andromeda, both being plants of the family Ericaceae and much attached to acidic soils. Andromeda is too big to consider for the alpine garden, but some forms of Cassiope certainly aren't and I commend them highly. "

Features Evergreen with dense, overlapping leaves and very dainty bell-shaped flowers.
Special Care If you can provide the specific growing conditions, they need

little attention. Remove any brown unkempt growths in spring.
Propagation Take semi-ripe cuttings in late summer or layer in spring.
Problems None.

Origin Alpine areas of north-east Asia.
Habit Dwarf sub-shrubs, similar to heathers in appearance.
Flowering Season Spring.
Size Mostly 10–30 x 30–40cm (4–12 x 12–16in).
Site Partial shade and moist, acidic soil; if this is not available, grow in a trough. Good choice for exposed sites or cool, open positions.
Best Grown Outdoors, in a rock garden.

Recommended Varieties
Cassiope 'Edinburgh' AGM one of easiest to grow, this dense erect bush arose as a chance seedling at Edinburgh Botanic Garden, slender dark green stems carry white flowers with contrasting red sepals and it is fairly tolerant of warm, dry conditions, 30 x 30cm (12 x 12in); C. lycopodiodes AGM prostrate emerald-green mat roughly 10 x 30cm (4 x 12in), in spring almost covered with small white flowers with red sepals, borne on red stalks, 'Beatrice Lilley' free-flowering variety and more compact than the species; C. tetragona upright plant reaching 30–45 x 30cm (12–18 x 12in) with four-cornered stems and open bell-like flowers.

Cerastium Alpine mouse-ear

" In common with most people, I find cerastiums and stellarias confusing. As seedlings, they are all but indistinguishable and most gardeners tend to call them all chickweed. To my mind, there isn't a good alpine species of Stellaria but there is one good Cerastium, and one that certainly justifies the overall common name applied to the genus – mouse-ears. They aren't neat and tidy plants so much be given room to sprawl and so display their particular charms. "

Origin Mountains and grassy uplands of Europe.
Habit Evergreen mats.
Flowering Season Late spring to early summer.
Size 10 x 30cm (4 x 12in).
Site Sun.
Best Grown Outdoors, in a rock garden, or in an alpine house.

Features Hardy mat of oval leaves with loose clusters of flowers.
Special Care Protect from damp winter weather.
Propagation Lift and divide plants after flowering.
Problems None.

Recommended Varieties
Cerastium alpinum var. lanatum has all its parts covered with white hairs.

Chamaedaphne
Leather leaf

" In a plant name, the prefix 'Chamae-' means close to the ground, or dwarf. Not surprisingly, it crops up in at least one alpine genus, this group of low-growing shrubs. The second bit of the name, however, is quite misleading: they aren't in any way related to Daphne, which means laurel, and even real daphnes aren't real laurels. So there you are – a nomenclatural hotchpotch, but a charming little plant nonetheless. "

Features Urn-shaped flowers.
Special Care Needs moist, acidic soil so mulching with conifer needles or sawdust will help.

Propagation Take semi-ripe cuttings in summer.
Problems None.

Origin Peat bogs and pond margins in temperate regions of Europe, Asia and North America.
Habit Evergreen sub-shrub.
Flowering Season Spring.
Size Dwarf form 30–45 x 75cm (12–18 x 30in).
Site Sun or partial shade and cool, peaty soil.
Best Grown Outdoors, in an acidic-soil bed.

Recommended Varieties
Chamaedaphne calyculata 'Nana' compact, free-flowering plant with glossy dark green leaves and white flowers.

Chamaedaphne calyculata 'Nana'

Chamaemelum Camomile

❝ *Here's another 'Chamae-' genus – low growing, like* Chamaedaphne, *but a herbaceous plant not a shrub. But what, you might wonder, is a low-growing '-melum'? From looking at the plant, you'd never guess; from smelling it, you might. It comes from the Latin and Greek melon, which means, would you believe, an apple. Yes, melons and chamaemelums are so called because they are supposed to smell like apples. In my garden,* Chamaemelum *smells like camomile, and a jolly good thing too.* ❞

Origin Grassy pastures and waste-lands of western Europe.
Habit Soft evergreen mats.
Flowering Season Summer.
Size 15-25 x 30–45cm (6–10 x 12–18in).
Site Full sun in a warm position and light, fertile, free-draining soil.
Best Grown Outdoors, in a rock garden.

Features Feathery, aromatic foliage and small daisy-like flowers.
Special Care Give a light dressing of general fertilizer in spring. Dead-head and cut back foliage to keep the plants compact.
Propagation Lift and divide plants in spring, or sow seed of species in summer.
Problems May be invasive.

Recommended Varieties
Chamaemelum nobile (syn. *Anthemis nobilis*) bright green leaves and white flowers with yellow centres, position carefully on rock gardens as it reaches 25 x 45cm (10 x 18in), 'Flore Pleno' has double, button-like flowers and makes an ideal edging as it is a neat 15 x 30cm (6 x 12in).

Chamaemelum nobile 'Flore Pleno'

PERENNIALS AND SHRUBS

Chiastophyllum Lamb's tail

Furry animals, or at least plant representations of them, are rather common in the garden: witness cat's paws, hare's ears and, here, lamb's tails. Chiastophyllum is a bit out of the usual run of alpine plants and is certainly worth growing for its distinctiveness, although it's an odd lamb that has a golden tail.

Origin Rocky woodlands of the Caucasus.
Habit Rosette-forming succulent.
Flowering Season Summer.
Size 15 x 30cm (6 x 12in).
Site Sun or partial shade in a sheltered site, and moist soil.
Best Grown Outdoors; ideal for crevices in a stone wall, a rock garden or the edge of a raised bed.

Special Care None.
Propagation Lift and divide plants after flowering, or take semi-ripe cuttings in summer.
Problems None.

> **Recommended Varieties**
> *Chiastophyllum oppositifolium* (syn. *C. simplicifolium*) AGM the only species, an unusual succulent alpine – its common name describes the yellow flower sprays, which droop at the tips and give the appearance of lamb's tails.

Chiastophyllum oppositifolium

Cortusa Alpine bells

I link Cortusa with Androsace. Both are in the primula family and both are different enough from primulas to have gained separate devotees. They fall into that group of alpine plants that are valuable for being partly shade tolerant.

Features Rosette of broad, lobed leaves and flowers held in umbels high above the foliage.
Special Care None.
Propagation Lift and divide plants after flowering. Sow seed either when ripe or in early spring.
Problems None.

Origin Central and south-eastern Europe, temperate Asia.
Habit Clump-forming herbaceous perennial.
Flowering Season Late spring to early summer.
Size 35 x 35cm (14 x 14in).
Site Light to moderate shade and cool, moist, loamy soil.
Best Grown Outdoors; ideal for the shaded edges of a rock garden.

> **Recommended Varieties**
> *Cortusa matthioli* easy to grow if you can recreate the required woodland conditions, foliage lies flat on the ground and leaves and stems are covered with rusty brown hairs, loose clusters of rich red-purple flowers are held high above the leaves on 35cm (14in) stalks.

Corydalis

Corydalis is one of those genera that has been in gardens for years, but it has really been the recent availability of the striking blue-flowered Himalayan species that has made folk realize just how attractive the familiar old yellow one is, too.

Features Attractive fern-like foliage and narrow, tubular flowers, sometimes with small spurs.
Special Care Tuberous types must be planted 5cm (2in) deep in autumn; they require more moisture in winter and a partial drying-out in summer.

Propagation All may be grown from fresh ripe seed, but the tuberous types take many years to flower, so it is quicker to lift and divide them in spring.

Problems Slugs; *C. lutea* can be invasive.

Origin Widely distributed in mountains of Europe and Asia.
Habit Herbaceous perennials, some species with fibrous roots, others tuberous.
Flowering Season Varies (see below).
Size Varies, but within the range 15–30 x 20–50cm (6–12 x 8–20in).
Site Partial shade and humus-rich soil.
Best Grown Outdoors, although some such as *C. cashmeriana* are difficult and better grown in an alpine house.

Corydalis flexuosa 'Purple Leaf'

Recommended Varieties
Corydalis cashmeriana Himalayan species highly prized for its bright sky-blue flowers in late spring or early summer and blue-green foliage, rhizomatous type requiring a cool, moist, lime-free soil and often thrives in colder gardens, rarely exceeds 15 x 25cm (6 x 10in) and difficult to re-establish after division; *C. flexuosa* loose clusters of pale to deep blue flowers appear above finely divided leaves from late spring to early summer, rhizomatous type and easy to grow, 30 x 30cm (12 x 12in); *C. lutea* (syn. *Pseudofumaria lutea*) easy-to-grow species with long-lasting yellow flowers that appear from spring, through summer and well into autumn, seeds itself around in walls, between paving and its spreading habit makes attractive ground cover, long tough tap-root so any unwanted plants must be pulled up at seedling stage, 20 x 50cm (8 x 20in); *C. solida* AGM spring-flowering species with pink, purple, red or white flowers and grey-green foliage, tuberous form that disappears from view in summer, 25 x 20cm (10 x 8in).

Crassula

❝ *You might expect to find crassulas in what is almost the opposite of the temperate rock garden: the cactus and succulent garden. It is true that most of them are plants of hot, dry places, but the few hardier types are worth including in a rock garden for the contrasting form and texture they bring.* ❞

Origin Southern Africa.
Habit Succulents with low rosettes or a bushy habit.
Flowering Season Summer.
Size *C. sarcocaulis* 30 x 30cm (12 x 12in), *C. milfordiae* 5 x 15cm (2 x 6in).
Site Full sun and protection from cold, as not fully hardy. Like other slightly tender rock garden plants, they will thrive best in soil that is fairly light and very free draining.
Best Grown As a pan plant in an alpine house.

Features Dense clusters of small flowers, but grown mainly for their foliage.
Special Care Most *Crassula* species are tender; those recommended below are among the hardiest but might not survive hard winters.
Propagation Sow seed in warmth in spring or take leaf cuttings in spring or summer.
Problems Aphids, mealybugs, vine weevil.

Recommended Varieties
Crassula milfordiae the low rosette of leaves is the main feature, being green in summer and bronzed in autumn and winter, in summer crimson buds open to produce dense clusters of tiny white flowers; *C. sarcocaulis* (syn. *Sedum sarcocaule*) deciduous sub-shrub whose fleshy stems become branched and woody with age, red buds open to tiny pale pink flowers that last all summer, alba has white flowers.

PERENNIALS AND SHRUBS

Crepis Hawksbeard

❝ *Beware the hawksbeard. It is plant that will seduce you at the garden centre but will then run riot in your garden and be with you forever. Or at least, it will if you choose unwisely. Far too many nurseries and garden centres still offer the brightly coloured but extremely invasive species, so make sure that you aren't seduced and buy only the types I recommend here.* ❞

Features Dandelion-like flowers.
Special Care None.
Propagation Lift and divide plants in spring. Sow seed in winter or early spring in a cold frame.
Problems None.

Origin Mountains of southern Europe.
Habit Clump-like habit or loose rosette of evergreen leaves.
Flowering Season Summer into autumn.
Size 20–30 x 20–30cm (8–12 x 8–12in).
Site Sunny position, and a good choice for poor, dry soil.
Best Grown Outdoors, in a large rock garden.

Cyananthus Trailing bellflower

❝ *Campanulas are usually, and understandably, called bellflowers. And there are trailing species, some of them very invasive, that could justifiably be called 'trailing bellflowers'. Generally, they aren't, the name being reserved for this close relative from the Himalayas, which is no less lovely and is much less vigorous.* ❞

Crepis aurea

Recommended Varieties
Most species are too weedy and invasive to be worth growing, but the following are exceptions: *Crepis aurea* (golden hawksbeard) variable species with the leaves and habit of a dandelion and flowers of copper-orange or bright yellow from summer into autumn, flower stems may range from 3cm (1¼in) to 25cm (10in) tall so choose those with shorter stems when buying; *C. incana* (pink dandelion) Greek species that forms a clump of hairy, grey leaves and carries branching stems of pink or purple flowers in summer, 20 x 20cm (8 x 8in).

Origin Himalayas, Tibet, south-western China.
Habit Herbaceous perennials with a low-growing, spreading habit.
Flowering Season Late summer to early autumn.
Size *C. delavayi* 10 x 20cm (4 x 8in), *C. lobatus* 10 x 40cm (4 x 16in), *C. microphyllus* 5 x 20cm (2 x 8in).
Site Partial shade and acidic soil that is moist and humus-rich.
Best Grown Outdoors, in a moist scree, acidic-soil bed or large trough.

Features The flowers resemble those of a periwinkle (*Vinca*).
Special Care It is worth improving the soil by digging in leaf mould. These plants are intolerant of hot, dry summers so tend to thrive better in wetter, cooler gardens.
Propagation Take softwood cuttings in late spring or early summer. Sow seed when ripe or in winter in pots in a cold frame.
Problems Slugs.

Recommended Varieties
Cyananthus delavayi species from south-western China with downy foliage and flowers; *C. lobatus* AGM found in low scrub and meadows in the Himalayas, prostrate with oval, pale green leaves and large blue flowers with hairy calyces, the shade of blue varies and the best colours are deep blue and purple-blue, 'Albus' is a white-flowered form; *C. microphyllus* AGM smaller species, more compact and with tiny thyme-like leaves, flowers are blue and have hairy calyces.

Cyclamen

❝ Hardy cyclamen are lovely but suffer from three drawbacks: some aren't as hardy as you might wish, even the more vigorous forms take several years to form a really attractive carpet, and all except one or two are rather expensive to buy. None of which should put off anyone from having at least a few in any alpine garden. ❞

Features Often heart-shaped leaves, and graceful flowers held well above the foliage on sturdy stems.
Special Care Do not disturb after planting.
Propagation Sow fresh seed as soon

as it is ripe or replant self-sown seedlings which form in abundance once plants are well established.
Problems Aphids, root eelworm, vine weevil, tuber rots, grey mould.

Origin Central and southern Europe, western Asia, northern Africa.
Habit Low-growing, herbaceous corm.
Flowering Season Varies (see below).
Size Mostly 6 x 15cm (2½ x 6in).
Site Partial shade; most soils suitable if not waterlogged.
Best Grown Outdoors, in a rock garden or large trough, for hardy species; others in an alpine house.

Cyclamen purpurascens

Recommended Varieties

Cyclamen balearicum scented species best grown in a shady part of an alpine house, leaves are pointed and marked with silver, flowers appear in mid-spring and are white with pink veins, 5 x 8cm (2 x 3in); *C. cilicium* AGM autumn-flowering species, grow outside in mild areas, otherwise in an alpine house, flowers are pink with a purple blotch at the petal bases and the oval leaves are deep green with cream markings, 7 x 13cm (2¾ x 5cm), f. *album* is pure white and comes true from seed; *C. coum* AGM valued for its winter flowers and ability to naturalize, very variable – leaves may be plain or patterned with either grey or silver and flowers may be pink, red or white, 6 x 15cm (2½ x 6in), f. *pallidum* 'Album' white flowers with a purple blotch at the base of the petals,

'Roseum' is well coloured; *C. cyprium* scented species for an alpine house, the white to pale pink flowers have a purple blotch at the base of the petals and appear from autumn to early winter, leaves are heart shaped with grey or silver markings and red undersides, 8 x 13cm (3 x 5in); *C. graecum* requires summer dormancy, it has long fleshy roots so grow in a deep pot or plant 10–15cm (4–6in) deep at the base of a sunny wall, the late-summer to autumn flowers are pink or red-purple with purple markings at the base of the petals, leaves are heart shaped and dark green often with grey or silver markings, 13 x 15cm (5 x 6in); *C. hederifolium* (syn. *C. neapolitanum*) well-known hardy cyclamen and one of the easiest to grow anywhere that is lightly shaded and cool, self-seeds freely, flowers are rose-

pink, sometimes white, and appear in late summer to mid-autumn, the heart-shaped leaves are variable but most have attractive markings, 15 x 23cm (6 x 9in); *C. libanoticum* AGM a species with large flowers that needs an alpine house in most areas, peppery-scented blooms are rose-pink with a red mark at the base of the petals and appear in late winter to early spring, heart-shaped leaves are green with red undersides, 8 x 15cm (3 x 6in), *C. mirabile* AGM similar to *C. cilicium* but leaves are often flushed with red and the petals are toothed 6 x 15cm (2½ x 6in); *C. purpurascens* (syn. *C. europaeum*) AGM hardy woodland cyclamen with scented, carmine-pink flowers that bloom from midsummer to early autumn, intolerant of drought so plant tubers deeply, 6 x 15cm (2½ x 6in).

Cytisus Broom

❝ *Broom is a name applied to several genera of shrubs. Many have their place in the garden although I think the genus* Cytisus *includes the best rock garden species. But do check carefully before you buy: none is suitable for a trough and some will be too big for all except the largest rock plantings.* ❞

Features The deciduous leaves are tiny and unremarkable, the main feature being the small pea-like flowers.
Special Care Easy to grow if the site and soil are correct. They tend to be short-lived shrubs, so it is worth propagating to obtain replacements. Lightly trim after flowering but take care not to cut into old wood.
Propagation Take semi-ripe cuttings in late summer, pinching out the growing tips when the young plants are about 25cm (10in) tall to ensure a bushy habit. Sow seed in spring or autumn.
Problems None, but they resent root disturbance.

Cytisus decumbens

Origin Varies, mostly Mediterranean.
Habit Prostrate shrubs.
Flowering Season Late spring to early summer.
Size Varies (see below).
Site Full sun, and ideal for poor, sandy soils.
Best Grown Outdoors, in a rock garden

Recommended Varieties

Cytisus ardoinoi AGM (Radon broom) grows on alkaline rocks in the French maritime Alps, a hummock-like shrub with arching branches bearing bright yellow flowers, 10–20 x 30–60cm (4–8 x 12–24in), *C. decumbens* (syn. *Genista decumbens*) prostrate broom from the southern Alps with wiry branching stems and brilliant yellow flowers, 10–30cm x 1m (4–12in x 3ft); *C. demissus* (syn.

Chamaecytisus hirsutus demissus) AGM lax, spreading plant from Greece, usually with pale yellow flowers, but named varieties are more compact and have more distinct flower colours, 8 x 20cm (3 x 8in); *C. purpureus* (syn. *Chamaecytisus purpureus*; purple broom) semi-erect shrub from south-eastern Europe with dark green leaves and pale pink to deep lilac flowers, 45 x 60cm (18 x 24in).

Daboecia Irish heath, St Dabeoc's heath

❝ *I have been conducting a campaign on behalf of* Daboecia *for many years. It is the unjustifiably ignored member of the heather family and has, I believe, the best flowers of all. Like most of its relatives, it has few really tiny forms, but several varieties are ideal for larger rock gardens on acidic soils.* ❞

Features Tiny leaves and small, pendent flowers.
Special Care Plant deeply and water well for the first growing season. Requires annual pruning to prevent plants from appearing unkempt. Cut back to the base of the dead flowers in spring.
Propagation Take shoot-tip cuttings in summer, or layer.
Problems Unsuitable soil leading to root rots.

Recommended Varieties

Daboecia cantabrica (syn. *D. polifolia*) fully hardy species with lavender flowers. There are many named forms with different flower colours: f. *alba* white-flowered form with bright green leaves, found in the wild in Connemara, hardier than the species and flowers well, 'Atropurpurea' is valued for its rich purple flowers, 'Bicolor' AGM white, pink and red flowers, sometimes striped, and mid-green leaves, 'Praegerae' very fine form from Connemara with deep cerise flowers and deciduous mid-green leaves.

Origin Western Europe excluding Britain but including Ireland.
Habit Dwarf, bushy, mostly evergreen shrubs.
Flowering Season Early summer and again in autumn.
Size 25–40 x 70cm (10–16 x 28in).
Site Open site in sun or partial shade, but avoid frost pockets. Acidic or neutral, moist but well-drained soil with plenty of humus.
Best Grown Outdoors, in a rock garden or acidic-soil bed for hardy species like *D. cantabrica*.

Daphne

❝ The two native British species of Daphne *are rather uncommon and are among the real prizes for any field botanist to discover in the wild. While they make good garden plants, we have to go to other parts of Europe, for the alpine types. They are miniature versions, but they do share their larger relatives' wonderful flower fragrance. ❞*

Origin Widespread, but most recommended here are from mountains of central and southern Europe.
Habit Deciduous or evergreen shrubs.
Flowering Season Late spring to early summer.
Size Most within the range 20–75 x 60–75cm (8–30 x 24–30in).
Site Partial shade and well-drained but fertile, humus-rich soil.
Best Grown Outdoors, in a rock garden.

Features Scented flowers and sometimes fruits.
Special Care Mulch with leaf mould to keep the roots cool. *D. cneorum* may be buried in summer so that only the leaf tips show, to produce a mat of foliage that will later be covered in flowers.

Propagation Take semi-ripe cuttings in summer, sow ripe seed or layer, but some species are difficult to propagate.
Problems Aphids, leaf spots, grey mould, viruses.

Daphne cneorum var. pygmaea

Recommended Varieties
D. alpina deciduous species from southern Europe, initially compact but eventually forms a loose open shrub, covered in late spring to early summer with scented white flowers, followed by orange-red fruit, 60 x 60cm (24 x 24in); *D. cneorum* (Garland flower) popular daphne valued for its scented, rose-pink flowers in late spring, the evergreen foliage is green with grey undersides, makes a low trailing shrub, 20 x 75cm (8 x 30in), 'Eximia' AGM widely grown for its vigour and large flowers, var. *pygmaea* very compact prostrate form from the Alps that grows very slowly to 10 x 30cm (4 x 12in); *D. x napolitana* AGM compact dense evergreen of garden origin, less hardy than most daphnes but the narrow, glossy dark green leaves and scented rose-pink flowers in late spring make it worth considering, 75 x 75cm (30 x 30in); *D. tangutica* Retusa Group (syn. *D. retusa*) AGM very hardy species from China and the Himalayas, evergreen with an upright habit and leathery leaves, the white and purple flowers are produced in terminal clusters and are very fragrant, bright red fruits sometimes follow flowering, 75 x 75cm (30 x 30in).

PERENNIALS AND SHRUBS

Dianthus Pinks

" *What greater contrast could there be between the gross, over-sized and often weirdly coloured objects that people insist on wearing in their buttonholes and the plants that I recommend here? The dwarf, alpine* Dianthus *species and varieties are a world away from their gross cousins, the florist's carnations.* "

Dianthus 'La Bourboule'

Origin Mostly southern and eastern Alps.

Habit Evergreen perennials.

Flowering Season Summer.

Size Most within the range 5–20 x 10–50cm (2–8 x 4–20in).

Site Open, sunny site and neutral or slightly alkaline soil. Tolerant of salt-winds and pollution.

Best Grown Outdoors, in a rock garden, edge of a border, raised bed or trough, or in an alpine house.

Features Most have grey-green or blue-grey foliage. The flowers are usually simple, with five petals, and many have a strong, spicy, clove-like scent.

Special Care Renew every three years as plants become woody with age.

Propagation Take cuttings (pipings) of non-flowering shoots in summer by pulling off the tips, which part, telescope fashion. Sow seed of species in autumn or winter and keep in a cold frame. Some of the tufted types may be divided after flowering or in spring.

Problems Aphids, roots aphids, rust, virus.

Recommended Varieties

D. alpinus (alpine pink) AGM easy but short-lived pink for a rock garden, native to limestone rocks in the south-eastern Alps, flowers are purple-red with paler spotting and borne above a loose cushion of narrow green leaves, 8 x 10cm (3 x 4in), 'Joan's Blood' AGM blood-red flowers with black centres and bronze foliage; *D. deltoides* (maiden pink) AGM popular species that self-seeds freely, forms a mat of dark green leaves with leafy stems bearing pink, red or white flowers, often with a darker eye, 20 x 30cm (8 x 12in), 'Albus' has white flowers and dark green foliage, 'Leuchtfunk' (syn. 'Flashing Light') has cerise flowers; *D. erinaceus* Turkish species that can be difficult to grow, needing plenty of sun otherwise flowering may be sparse, forms a neat cushion of stiff prickly leaves with star-like pink flowers, 5 x 50cm (2 x 20in); *D. gratianopolitanus* (syn. *D. caesius*, Cheddar pink) AGM somewhat variable native British species so choose neat low-growing plants, forms a lax tuft of grey-green leaves and fragrant, pale pink flowers on long slender stems, 15 x 40cm (6 x 16in); *D.* 'Inshriach Dazzler' AGM compact alpine pink with carmine-red flowers with fringed petals and buff undersides, 15 x 20cm (6 x 8in); *D.* 'La Bourboule' AGM compact alpine pink producing scented clear pink flowers with fringed petals, 'La Bourboule Albus' is a white-flowered form, 15 x 20cm (6 x 8in); *D. myrtinervius* more compact relation of *D. deltoides* from the Balkans, northern Greece and Macedonia, grows to form a dense mat of bright green leaves and in summer is covered with deep pink flowers, each with a paler eye, 5 x 20cm (2 x 8in); *D.* 'Nyewoods Cream' grey-green mat of foliage and cream flowers, 15 x 20cm (6 x 8in); *D. pavonius* (syn. *D. neglectus*) AGM pink flowers above a mat of grey-green leaves in summer, 8 x 20cm (3 x 8in); *D.* 'Pikes Pink' AGM compact alpine pink with scented, pale pink semi-double flowers and blue-green foliage, 15 x 20cm (6 x 8in).

Dicentra Bleeding heart

" Dicentras are those improbable relatives of the poppies that always seem rather too artificial to be true species. The larger types are an acquired taste in the woodland garden; the smaller species are an acquired taste in the alpine garden. "

Origin Mountain woodlands, *D. cucullaria* eastern North America.
Habit Clump-forming rhizomatous or tuberous perennials.
Flowering Season Spring.
Size 20–30 x 25–45cm (8–12 x 10–18in).
Site Partial shade and gritty soil enriched with humus.
Best Grown Outdoors, in a shady rock garden.

Features Nodding flowers, sometimes with spurs.
Special Care *D. cucullaria* is dormant over the summer and should be kept dry.
Propagation Sow ripe seed, or lift and divide plants in early spring.
Problems Slugs.

Recommended Varieties
Dicentra 'Bountiful' rhizomatous plant with purple-pink flowers in late spring, 30 x 45cm (12 x 18in); *D. cucullaria* (Dutchman's breeches) compact tuberous plant with fern-like grey-green foliage and white flowers tipped with yellow, 20 x 25cm (8 x 10in).

Dodecatheon American cowslip, Shooting stars

" I have been slightly uncharitable about some plants in the primula family, implying that they are less subtle relatives of the real thing. But with these members of the same group, I am happy to be very complimentary. They certainly don't look like primulas, although the leaves might be a reminder, but in their swept-back flowers they don't need to for they have a charm and character all their own. "

Features Basal rosette of foliage and cyclamen-like flowers on long stems.
Special Care None.
Propagation Sow ripe seed, then expose to cold to trigger germination.

Origin Western North America.
Habit Clump-forming herbaceous perennials.
Flowering Season Late spring.
Size 20–35 x 15–25cm (8–14 x 6–10in).
Site Shade and moist soil.
Best Grown Outdoors, in a rock garden or large trough.

Recommended Varieties
D. dentatum AGM dainty white flowers borne on slender stems, on close examination dark purple anthers may be seen and sometimes spotting of the petal bases, 20 x 20cm (8 x 8in); *D. jeffreyi* Californian species with deep red-purple flowers and deep purple stamens, flowers appear from late spring to early summer, 30 x 25cm (12 x 10in); *D. pulchellum* (syn. *D. amethystinum*, *D. pauciflorum* of gardens, *D. radicatum*) AGM a mass of deep cerise-pink flowers appears in mid- to late spring, 35 x 15cm (14 x 6in).

Lift and divide plants in spring.
Problems Slugs, snails.

Dodecatheon dentatum

PERENNIALS AND SHRUBS

Draba Whitlow grass

❝ *The whitlow grass isn't a grass, it's a member of the brassica family, a relationship betrayed by their characteristic cross-shaped flowers. They are charming, but not as easy or robust as you might expect from this family.* ❞

Origin Mountains of Europe.
Habit Evergreen or semi-evergreen mat, cushion or hummock.
Flowering Season Late spring.
Size 5–10 x 20–25cm (2–4 x 8–10in).
Site Full sun and gritty compost.
Best Grown Outdoors, in troughs or raised beds, or in pans in an alpine house.

Features Pretty four-petalled flowers.
Special Care Protect from excessive winter rain, and in an alpine house water carefully to avoid cold water lying on the foliage.
Propagation Sow seed in a cold frame in autumn.
Problems Aphids, red spider mite.

Recommended Varieties
Draba aizoides semi-evergreen with a mat or cushion of deep green leaves and bright yellow flowers, found in rocky or stony mountains often on limestone, 10 x 25cm (4 x 10in); *D. rigida* var. *imbricata* compact form of a very pretty species from eastern Turkey, a cushion of overlapping bristly leaves topped with golden-yellow flowers on 12cm (5in) stems, 5 x 20cm (2 x 8in).

Dryas Mountain avens

❝ *This plant has been very dear to me since I first found it growing in the Scottish Highlands. It isn't a common British plant and so seeing in it the wild was a real privilege. I have grown it in my rock gardens ever since but it does need space, because despite the lovely leaves and flowers it can become unkempt and sprawling.* ❞

Origin Mountainous areas of the northern hemisphere.
Habit Prostrate evergreen sub-shrubs.
Flowering Season Late spring to early summer.
Size 10 x 90cm (4 x 36in).
Site Full sun and flowers best in poor soil.
Best Grown Outdoors, in a large rock garden, gravel garden or over a ledge.

Dryas octopetala

Features Carpet of oak-like leaves and large white flowers that turn to follow the sun. Ideal plants for covering a large sunny rock garden or front of a border.
Special Care Easy to grow; may be kept in check by clipping back after flowering.
Propagation Take semi-ripe cuttings in summer, sow ripe seed in late summer or autumn, or lift and transplant rooted stems in spring.
Problems None.

Recommended Varieties
D. drummondii North American species with nodding pale yellow bells in early summer; *D. octopetala* AGM north European species, rather rare in Britain, with upward-facing cup-like flowers that are white with yellow centres, fluffy seedheads add autumn interest, 'Minor' is a more compact form, worth searching out for its value in small rock gardens; *D. x suendermannii* AGM hybrid between the two species above, slightly nodding cup-shaped flowers of creamy yellow appear from spring to early summer.

Edraianthus Grassy bells

❝ *Unless you are familiar with that rather rampant border perennial Campanula glomerata, you might not immediately connect this species with the genus Campanula. But, in truth, in its colour and inflorescence shape it is a scaled-down, less vigorous version.* ❞

Edraianthus graminifolius

Origin Rocky mountain meadows of the Mediterranean.
Habit Evergreen or herbaceous tufts.
Flowering Season Summer.
Size *E. graminifolius* 15 x 15cm (6 x 6in), *E. pumilio* 3 x 15cm (1¼ x 6in).
Site Sun and light soil, preferably alkaline.
Best Grown Outdoors, in a rock garden, scree, dry wall or trough. May be also be grown in an alpine house.

Features Grass-like foliage and *Campanula*-like flowers.
Special Care Resting buds are vulnerable to winter wet.
Propagation Sow seed in a cold frame in autumn or take semi-ripe cuttings in midsummer, although wild-collected seed of *E. graminifolius* produces variable seedlings.
Problems Outdoors, slugs and snails; in an alpine house, also aphids and red spider mite.

Recommended Varieties
Edraianthus graminifolius AGM a cluster of purple-blue bells is held just above tufts of leaf rosettes; *E. pumilio* (syn. *Wahlenbergia pumilio*) AGM tiny cushion of foliage covered with upturned bells of pale to deep violet from early to late summer.

Epilobium Willowherb

❝ *Not many gardeners willingly embrace willowherbs in their affections, especially if their garden is host to that introduced monster,* Epilobium angustifolium, *the rosebay willowherb. But be prepared to investigate this very large genus rather more thoroughly and you will find some very charming little species, all with the same elongated tubular flowers in a rather shocking pink.* ❞

Epilobium dodonaei

Origin *E. dodonaei* Alps and Apennines, *E. glabellum* New Zealand, *E. obcordatum* southwestern United States.
Habit Herbaceous perennials of variable habit.
Flowering Season Midsummer until early autumn.
Size Varies, but around 25 x 20cm (10 x 8in).
Site Sun or partial shade; tolerates most soil, except waterlogged sites.
Best Grown Outdoors, in a rock garden.

Features Small, four-petalled flowers and silky seeds.
Special Care None.
Propagation Lift and divide plants in spring, take semi-ripe cuttings in spring, or sow seed in spring or autumn.
Problems Slugs, snails, rust, powdery mildew.

Recommended Varieties
E. dodonaei spreading perennial with a woody rootstock, found in the wild on rocks and gravel, grey-green hairy leaves and cup-shaped flowers of rose-pink from early to midsummer, requires gravelly or sandy soil for the neatest habit, 25 x 25cm (10 x 10in); *E. glabellum* semi-evergreen species, best in full sun but tolerates some shade, with cream or pink flowers borne in succession from midsummer to early autumn, makes good ground cover, 20 x 40cm (8 x 16in); *E. obcordatum* wiry, spreading stems and rose-pink flowers, 15 x 25cm (6 x 10in).

PERENNIALS AND SHRUBS

Eranthis Winter aconite

❝ *I've already recommended* Adonis *because it looks like a winter aconite. I'm now going to recommend the real thing, but only if you have a large rock garden with room for it to spread. In confined space, on most garden soils, you will be forever pulling out its self-sown seedlings.* ❞

Features Cup-shaped flowers that sit on a 'ruff' of foliage.
Special Care Plant tubers 5cm (2in) deep in autumn.
Propagation Lift and divide plants in spring after flowering; much less successful when divided as dormant tubers. Sow seed in containers in a cold frame in late spring.
Problems None.

Origin Damp woodlands of Europe and Asia, *E. hyemalis* southern France to Bulgaria.
Habit Clump-forming tuberous perennial.
Flowering Season Late winter to early spring.
Size Each plant only 5–8 x 5cm (2–3 x 2in), but self-seeds readily to form a large carpet.
Site Partial shade and moist but well-drained loam; thrives on alkaline soils but unaccountably difficult to establish in some gardens whereas in others, apparently similar, it can be invasive.
Best Grown Outdoors, beneath deciduous shrubs or allowed to naturalize.

Recommended Varieties
Eranthis hyemalis AGM bright, shiny yellow flowers appear from late winter onwards above a ruff of bright green leaves, Tubergenii Group is a range of sterile hybrids between *E. hyemalis* and *E. cilicica* with larger, later flowers.

Erigeron Fleabane

❝ *To many gardeners,* Erigeron *is a genus of rather tall border daisies, or a wonderful little freely spreading Mexican species called* Erigeron karvinskianus. *Neither is right for the rock garden, but there are still others that are. They retain all that daisy family charm but on a small, disciplined scale.* ❞

Features Basal cluster of often hairy leaves, and daisy-like flowers.
Special Care Dead-head when practicable to promote further flowering. Cut back to the ground in autumn and protect from winter wet.
Propagation Lift and divide plants in

Origin Dry grasslands and mountains of North America and Europe.
Habit Varies greatly, from tall border perennials to clump-forming, mat-like or hummock plants.
Flowering Season Summer.
Size Varies greatly (see below).
Site Sunny, but light shade is tolerated. Soil should be fertile and well drained but not dry in summer.
Best Grown Outdoors, in a rock garden or in and around paving.

Erigeron alpinus

late spring. Replant self-sown seedlings or sow seed in a cold frame in spring.
Problems Slugs.

Recommended Varieties
Erigeron alpinus from meadows and rocky mountains of northern Europe, slender stems bear mauve-pink flowers with yellow centres during summer, 25 x 20cm (10 x 8in), *E. aurantiacus* rather large alpine from Turkestan that reaches 30 x 30cm (12 x 12in) but is worth including in a large rock garden for its rich orange flowers; *E. aureus* North American species with a mound-like habit of grey-green leaves and, in summer, golden-yellow daisy flowers, 5–10 x 15cm (2–4 x 6in); *E. compositus* another North American species, forming a loose cushion of grey-green leaves with blue, pink or white flowers, 15 x 10cm (6 x 4in).

Erica Heather, heath

❝ Erica is the most versatile of the half dozen or so genera that might loosely be called heaths or heathers. It is the largest in number of species; it is the largest in number of varieties; and it is the genus that includes some of the best of the smaller forms for the rock garden. It also uniquely offers you the option of growing heathers if you don't have an acidic soil. ❞

Origin Europe, Cape Province of South Africa.

Habit Evergreen sub-shrubs.

Flowering Season Summer or winter.

Size Most in the range 30–50 x 50–75cm (12–20 x 20–30in).

Site Full sun to partial shade. Soil should be free draining and acidic for most types, although *E. carnea* and *E. x darleyensis* are lime tolerant. Ideal for exposed sites.

Best Grown Outdoors, in a rock garden, although very small varieties can be grown in a trough.

Erica erigena 'Golden Lady'

Features Narrow, needle-like leaves that occur in colourful shades of green or yellow, many having winter tints. Small flowers, usually in pink, purple, red or white but very colourful en masse.

Special Care Mulch with an acidic material such as pine needles. A balanced general or rose fertilizer may be given in spring. Regular annual trimming after flowering (easiest with single-handed shears) prevents the plants from becoming leggy.

Propagation Take semi-ripe cuttings in early summer. Plants may also be layered in late summer or autumn.

Problems None.

Recommended Varieties

Erica carnea (syn. *E. herbacea*) varieties are winter-flowering heathers that tolerate lime: 'Ann Sparkes' AGM orange and yellow foliage with red tips in spring, deep red flowers, spreads to 25cm (10in), 'Foxhollow' AGM vivid golden-yellow foliage that becomes more intense in winter and develops red tints, sparse pale pink flowers, 'King George' bright rose-pink flowers, 'Myretoun Ruby' AGM crimson flowers, one of the best reds, 'Pink Spangles' AGM shell-pink flowers that deepen as they age, trailing habit, 'Springwood White', AGM bright green foliage, white flowers, trailing habit to 60cm (24in), 'Vivellii' AGM deep green-bronze foliage, dark red flowers; *E. cinerea* varieties are summer- and autumn-flowering heathers that require an acidic soil: 'Alba Minor' AGM bright green foliage, white flowers, compact, 'Eden Valley' AGM mid-green foliage, lavender and white flowers, 'Pink Ice' AGM only 15cm (6in) tall but spreads to 35cm (14in), clear rose-pink flowers; *E. x darleyensis* varieties flower between winter and spring and are moderately lime tolerant: 'Arthur Johnson' AGM green foliage with cream tips in spring, long spikes of slightly scented pink flowers, 'Furzey' AGM very dark green foliage with pink tips in spring, rose-pink flowers, 'Ghost Hills' AGM light green foliage with cream tips in spring, 'Jack H. Brummage' golden-yellow leaves in summer, orange-bronze in winter, mauve-pink flowers; *E. erigena* (syn. *E. hibernica*, *E. mediterranea*) spring flowers, moderately lime tolerant, 'Golden Lady' AGM carpeting habit, bright yellow foliage, sparse white flowers, scorched by cold winds, 30 x 40cm (12 x 16in), 'W. T. Rackcliff' AGM bright green foliage, white flowers, 75 x 60cm (30 x 24in); *E. tetralix* 'Con Underwood' needs a moist acidic soil, hummock forming, grey-green foliage, red flowers in summer or autumn; *E. vagans* varieties have summer to autumn flowers and are moderately lime tolerant: 'Lyonesse' AGM bright green foliage, white flowers, 'Mrs D. F. Maxwell' AGM dark green foliage, light rose-pink flowers.

PERENNIALS AND SHRUBS

Erinus Fairy foxglove

❝ *A colleague who some years ago was making a television programme about alpine plants said that this was the plant at the top of the list he told the producer they would have to include. Although I'm not sure that this is the archetypal alpine species, it does seem to include many of the more important features – although sadly, I find it short lived.* ❞

Origin Mostly Africa, *E. alpinus* Europe.
Habit Semi-evergreen perennials.
Flowering Season Late spring to summer.
Size 8 x 10cm (3 x 4in).
Site Full sun to partial shade and light, reasonably fertile soil.
Best Grown Outdoors; self-seeds freely so ideal for old stone walls.

Features Masses of two-lipped tubular flowers.

Erinus alpinus

Special Care None.
Propagation Sow seed in spring or autumn, or take softwood cuttings in spring.
Problems None.

> **Recommended Varieties**
> *Erinus alpinus* tuft of sticky leaves and pink, purple or white flowers, var. *albus* white flowers, 'Mrs Charles Boyle' pure pink flowers.

Erodium Stork's bill

❝ *Just as not many people refer to geraniums as cranesbills, so fewer refer to their relatives erodiums as stork's bills. In truth, rather fewer people grow them, which is a shame because, while it is a genus far smaller and less dramatic than* Geranium, *it does include several small enough for the alpine garden.* ❞

Origin Rocky habitats on mostly alkaline mountains; almost cosmopolitan, although those recommend below are from Europe.
Habit Sub-shrubs.
Flowering Season Summer.
Size Varies (see below).
Site Sunny, warm site and gritty soil; tolerant of alkaline soils.
Best Grown Outdoors, in a rock garden.

Features Attractive foliage and characteristic spirally twisted fruit.
Special Care None.
Propagation Sow ripe seed in a cold frame in autumn. Lift and divide plants in spring, or take basal cuttings in late spring or early summer.
Problems None.

> **Recommended Varieties**
> *Erodium chrysanthum* very pretty Greek species with attractive, finely divided silver foliage and unusual pale yellow flowers from late spring to early summer, male and female flowers on separate plants, 15 x 40cm (6 x 16in); *E. guttatum* rather large for a rock plant at 15 x 60cm (6 x 24in) but flowers well over a long period, grey-green foliage is heart shaped and covered in soft hairs, the white flowers have attractive dark blotches and are borne from early summer to early autumn; *E. reichardii* (syn. *E. chamaedryoides*) barely hardy species, tolerating down to -5°C (23°F), from Majorca and Corsica but worth growing if you have a warm sunny position, very neat at only 7 x 15cm (2¾ x 6in) so ideal for a trough, the saucer-shaped flowers are white with red veins and nestle among the heart-shaped leaves.

Erysimum

❝ *The genus* Erysimum *is the new home for wallflowers, which were called* Cheiranthus, *and although the traditional fragrant spring wallflower of cottage gardens is too large a plant for the alpine garden, there are several species and varieties much smaller in stature that do make very attractive additions.* ❞

Features Characteristic four-petalled cross-shaped flowers, mostly in shades of yellow.
Special Care Trim lightly after flowering.
Propagation Seed sow in a cold frame in spring, or take softwood cuttings in spring or summer.

Recommended Varieties
Erysimum capitatum small species from the western United States with clusters of pale yellow flowers from late spring to midsummer, 25cm (10in) tall; *E. helveticum* (syn. *E. pumilum*) small tufted plant with grey-green foliage and lemon-yellow flowers, main flowering display from mid-spring to midsummer but flowers appear on and off throughout the year, Pyrenees and Alps, up to 25cm (10in) tall; *E. hieraciifolium* (syn. *E. alpinum*) Scandinavian species, very neat, only 15cm (6in) tall with scented flowers of pale yellow; *E.* 'Jubilee Gold' bushy evergreen perennial with golden-yellow flowers in mid- to late spring, 40 x 45cm (16 x 18in); *E. linifolium* woody evergreen perennial that forms a mat of grey-green foliage and has long stems bearing lilac or lavender-blue flowers needs a warm, sheltered site to protect it from frost, 12 x 25cm (5 x 10in); *E.* 'Moonlight' evergreen mat of foliage covered with primrose-yellow flowers in early spring to early summer, 25 x 45cm (10 x 18in); *E. mutabile* similar to *E. linifolium* but with different flower colours on the same plant, ranging from pale yellow and buff to mauve-purple, 12 x 25cm (5 x 10in).

Problems Mildew, leaf spots, flea beetles.

Origin Widespread, including Europe, North America, northern Africa and Asia, on well-drained, alkaline soils.
Habit Mostly woody evergreen perennials.
Flowering Season Varies from spring to summer.
Size Varies within the range 12–40 x 25–45cm (5–16 x 10–18in).
Site Full sun and neutral or alkaline soil.
Best Grown Outdoors, in a rock garden.

Frankenia Sea heath

❝ *Frankenia is a good example of the fact that, in some ways, plants of the seashore and plants of the mountains have things in common. Most particularly, they tend to be tolerant of strong winds and prefer well-drained soils. The coastal species, however, are generally less hardy, although also less prone to damage from clinging damp.* ❞

Features These plants look superficially like heathers.
Special Care Very free-draining soil and protection from cold winds are essential.
Propagation Lift and divide plants after flowering, or take semi-ripe cuttings in summer.
Problems None.

Frankenia thymifolia

Origin Coastal areas in the northern hemisphere, *F. laevis* southern Britain, Europe and western Asia, *F. thymifolia* Spain and north-western Africa.
Habit Evergreen sub-shrubs or perennials.
Flowering Season Mid- to late summer.
Size 8cm x 1m (3in x 3ft).
Site Sun and light soil; tolerant of salt.
Best Grown Outdoors, in a rock garden or large trough.

Recommended Varieties
Frankenia laevis prostrate species with red-brown wiry stems and pink flowers; *F. thymifolia* low, tufted mat of triangular grey leaves, with clusters of tiny pink flowers in summer.

PERENNIALS AND SHRUBS

Gentiana Gentian

❝ *I mentioned earlier that Erinus was top of a friend's list of alpine plants. If I had to name the plant that most people think is the most typical, however, the gentian would be close to the top of the selection. Gentians are much-loved plants in a genus larger than is generally appreciated. However, many are far from easy; and some are extremely difficult.* **❞**

Features Despite the wide range in plant form and shape, the flowers are constant in their elongated trumpets.
Special Care It is essential to check soil and site requirements carefully.
Propagation Varies. Sow seed or lift and divide G. acaulis, both in autumn, or take semi-ripe cuttings in late summer. G. asclepiadea is raised easily from seed sown in spring or autumn. G. farreri may be divided in spring but establishment is uncertain; take softwood cuttings in summer; seed sown in autumn germinates fairly readily, but seldom comes true. Lift and divide Asian hybrids in early spring. G. septemfida is best propagated from seed sown in autumn or semi-ripe cuttings taken in early summer. Propagate G. sino-ornata by sowing seed or lifting and dividing , both in autumn; alternatively, take semi-ripe cuttings in late summer. G. verna may be raised from seed sown in autumn, but this is difficult as seedling roots are easily damaged.
Problems Slugs, snails, rust.

Gentiana x macauleyi 'Kingfisher'

Recommended Varieties
G. acaulis (syn. G. kochiana; trumpet gentian) AGM very well-known plant from European mountains, but difficult to bring into flower, the intense blue flowers with internal markings appear from spring to early summer above a flat evergreen mat of foliage, 8 x 30cm (3 x 12in); G. asclepiadea (willow gentian) AGM arching stems and long narrow leaves make this a graceful species (and very easy to raise from seed), flowers are azure-blue with attractive markings within the trumpets, flowering starts in midsummer and continues until early autumn, eastern Europe and western Asia, 60 x 45cm (24 x 18in); G. farreri Tibetan species that is semi-evergreen with trailing stems of bright green leaves, the pale blue flowers appear in early autumn, with attractive markings inside the trumpets, 7 x 30cm (2¾ x 12in); G. 'Inverleith' AGM one of the best Asian hybrids, semi-evergreen rosettes of foliage and prostrate stems bearing pale blue flowers with darker stripes in autumn, 10 x 30cm (4 x 12in); G. x macauleyi AGM hybrid of G. sino-ornata and G. farreri and similar to the former, mid- to deep blue flowers and long narrow leaves, 'Kingfisher' is a good, more compact form at 5 x 30cm (2 x 12in); G. septemfida AGM Asian species with bell-shaped blue or blue-purple flowers in late summer, easy to grow in most soils but variable in habit and flower colour, 20 x 30cm (8 x 12in), var. lagodechiana form from the eastern Caucasus with prostrate stems and usually only one flower per stem; G. sino-ornata AGM one of the best of all alpines but it isn't always easy to satisfy its growing conditions, semi-evergreen with prostrate stems bearing upright flowers of rich blue from early to late autumn, the flowers lie on the ground and stems root where they touch, south-western China, 7 x 15–30cm (2¾ x 6–12in), variants include 'Angel's Wings', blue flowers with white markings, and 'Brin Form', long flower stalks and scrambling habit; G. verna (spring gentian, star gentian) evergreen low mat or tuft supports sky-blue flowers in spring to early summer, Alps, Ireland and Russia, 4 x 10cm (1½ x 4in).

Origin Asia, Europe.

Habit Evergreen, mat- or clump-forming perennials.

Flowering Season Varies from spring through summer to autumn, depending on species.

Size Varies greatly (see below).

Site *G. acaulis* full sun and well-drained but fertile, humus-rich soil, *G. asclepiadea* partial shade and moist, acidic soil, *G. farreri* tolerates lime, *G. septemfida* full sun but tolerant of most soils, *G. sino-ornata* moist, deep, lime-free soil, in warm dry areas it is better in partial shade, *G. verna* full sun and light, free-draining soil.

Best Grown Outdoors, in a rock garden; *G. verna* is ideal for troughs but resents disturbance.

Geranium

❝ Geranium is arguably the most valuable genus of hardy ornamental plants. Among the many species are several that grow naturally in rocky, mountainous areas, just the type of place that you would expect to find a good alpine; and so you do. ❞

Features Easy to grow, and an attractive combination of pretty foliage and saucer-shaped flowers.

Special Care None.

Propagation Lift and divide plants in spring or autumn. Species come true from seed sown in spring or autumn, and *Geranium dalmaticum* is readily propagated from root cuttings.

Problems None.

Geranium orientalitibeticum

Origin *G. dalmaticum* rocky places in south-western former Yugoslavia and Albania, *G. farreri* and *G. pylzowianum* western China, *G. orientalitibeticum* south-western China.

Habit Mat-forming or low-growing herbaceous perennials.

Flowering Season Summer.

Size Most 10 x 25cm (4 x 10in).

Site Open, sunny site necessary for the best flowers; soil should be moderately fertile.

Best Grown Most outdoors, in a trough or scree, although *G. farreri* is best grown in a pot in an alpine house.

Recommended Varieties
Geranium cinereum 'Ballerina' AGM hybrid between *G. cinereum* var. *cinereum* and subsp. *subcaulescens*, long flowering season and purple-pink flowers with darker veins above neat grey-green foliage, 'Lawrence Flatman' is similar but more vigorous, with the petals having a dark mark towards the apex; *G. dalmaticum* AGM neat cushion with glossy, aromatic foliage that is often attractively tinted in autumn and shell-pink or white flowers, a valuable plant as it will thrive in very thin, poor soil, 'Album' is white with a slight pink tint; *G. farreri* (syn. *G. napuligerum*) in late spring flowers of the palest pink with prominent blue-black anthers appear above a low dome of foliage, 10–15cm (4–6in) high; *G. orientalitibeticum* (syn. *G. stapfianum* var. *roseum*) deep pink flowers with a white centre, the foliage is especially lovely and has yellow marbling, spreads by underground tubers so can swamp other plants, 20–40cm x 1m (8–16in x 3ft); *G. pylzowianum* deep rose-pink flowers with darker veins and prettily patterned leaves, flowers in late spring or early summer and then becomes dormant until the following spring, spreads by underground runners and tiny tubers, 15–25 x 25cm (6–10 x 10in).

PERENNIALS AND SHRUBS

Geum Avens

❝ *I always think geums are rather undistinguished plants, mainly because I find that the flowers on the border perennials are really too small in relation to the size of the leaves. The smaller, rock garden varieties seem to be better proportioned, however; the leaves and flowers have a better size balance, and so individually the plants are more attractive.* ❞

Origin All those recommended below are from mountains of central and/or southern Europe.
Habit Clump-forming herbaceous perennials.
Flowering Season Summer.
Size 15–30 x 30cm (6–12 x 12in).
Site Full sun and fertile soil.
Best Grown Outdoors, in a rock garden.

Features Easy to grow, with attractive bowl-shaped flowers.
Special Care None.
Propagation Lift and divide in spring or autumn. Species may be raised from seed sown in autumn or spring.
Problems Sawfly larvae.

Recommended Varieties
Geum 'Borisii' (syn. *G. coccineum*) hybrid between *G. bulgaricum* and *G. reptans* that occurs in the wild in Bulgaria, striking orange-yellow flowers in summer, *G. montanum* (alpine avens) AGM forms a leafy clump bearing golden-yellow flowers in summer; *G. x rhaeticum* hybrid between two southern European species, *G. montanum* and *G. reptans*, with large, brilliant orange flowers.

Gypsophila

❝ Gypsophila *conjures up an image of a florist's bouquet with tiny white flowers dotted among the other ingredients. But there is more to* Gypsophila *than* G. paniculata *'Bristol Fairy', which serves the floristry trade. Among many others are some neat and pretty alpines with very different flowers.* ❞

Origin *G. aretioides* northern Iran and Caucasus, *G. cerastioides* Himalayas, *G. repens* central, southern and eastern Europe.
Habit Mat- or cushion-like herbaceous perennials.
Flowering Season Mostly summer.
Size 5-20 x 15-30cm (2-8 x 6-12in).
Site Full sun and ideally gritty alkaline or neutral soil, although *G. cerastioides* grows better in humus-rich soil.
Best Grown Outdoors, in a rock garden, although *G. aretioides* is often grown successfully in an alpine house.

Features Narrow grey-green leaves and small five-petalled flowers.
Special Care Intolerant of winter wet.
Propagation Sow seed in spring or autumn, or take root cuttings in late autumn or winter.
Problems Stem rot.

Recommended Varieties
Gypsophila aretioides compact cushion of tiny leaves with white, stemless flowers in early summer, 'Caucasica' forms a very dense cushion of minute rosettes; *G. cerastioides* loose mat of semi-evergreen leaves, loose panicles of white flowers streaked with purple borne on 10cm (4in) stems from late spring to midsummer; *G. repens* semi-evergreen mat of grey-green leaves with white or pink flowers, 'Dorothy Teacher' good, more compact form with blue-green leaves and rose-pink flowers all summer.

Geum borisii

Haberlea

There's an old maxim that rock gardens and shade don't mix. However, this can unfortunately put off many people from creating a rock garden where, given a sensible choice of plants, one would succeed perfectly well. In a more deeply shaded spot or at one end of a long rock garden, Haberlea is one of the plants that your rock garden would need, and it invariably appears on any list I give of plants for a shaded garden, rocky or not.

Origin Shaded rocky areas of the Balkans.
Habit Herbaceous perennials.
Flowering Season Spring to early summer.
Size 15 x 25cm (6 x 10in).
Site Partial shade and moist, acidic or neutral soil enriched with humus.
Best Grown In an alpine house, or outdoors in crevices in a wall or between rocks. May also be grown in an acidic-soil bed.

Features Basal rosette of scalloped leaves and nodding, trumpet-like flowers borne on long stalks.
Special Care Protect from winter wet and cold winds, and avoid root disturbance.
Propagation Sow seed in spring or lift and divide plants in spring or autumn.
Problems Slugs, snails.

Recommended Varieties
Haberlea rhodopensis AGM dense rosette of scalloped leaves covered in soft hairs and violet-blue flowers from spring to early summer, 'Virginalis' has pure white flowers that contrast with the dark foliage.

Haberlea rhodopensis

Hacquetia

Although botanically unrelated and only brought together by alphabetic chance, Hacquetia very often follows Haberlea in plant lists because both are shade tolerant and low growing. Just as Haberlea is an indispensable addition to the shaded rock garden, therefore, so is Hacquetia.

Origin Woodlands in central Europe.
Habit Clump-forming rhizomatous perennial.
Flowering Season Late winter to early spring.
Size 5–15 x 15–30cm (2–6 x 6–12in).
Site Shady site and acidic or neutral soil that is moist but well drained and enriched with humus.
Best Grown Outdoors, in a lightly shaded rock garden or acidic-soil bed.

Features Tiny flowers surrounded by a ruff of bracts.
Special Care None, but self-seeds freely once established.
Propagation Sow ripe seed in autumn and leave in a cold frame over winter. Lift and divide plants in spring, or take root cuttings in winter.
Problems Slugs and snails.

Recommended Varieties
Hacquetia epipactis (syn. *Dondia epipactis*) AGM golden-yellow flowers are surrounded by shiny green bracts and appear early, usually before the glossy, bright green leaves.

Hacquetia epipactis

PERENNIALS AND SHRUBS

Hebe

❝ I have grown hebes in each of my gardens over the years, but I have made mistakes. I have planted species that grew far larger than I expected and I have planted varieties that proved much less hardy than I had been promised. I have every confidence that those I recommend here will not let you down on either of these counts. ❞

Origin New Zealand.
Habit Evergreen shrubs in a range of sizes.
Flowering Season Mostly summer.
Size Varies greatly, but those recommended below are within the range 20–45 x 30–90cm (8–18 x 12–36in).
Site Full sun essential, but tolerant of most soils if not wet over winter. Ideal for coastal areas or other windy but mild sites.
Best Grown Outdoors, in a rock garden.

Features Varying leaf colours and textures, some with attractive inflorescences of small flowers.
Special Care None.
Propagation Take semi-ripe cuttings in late summer.
Problems Leaf spot and downy mildew in damp conditions.

Recommended Varieties
Hebe buchananii compact but spreading species with leathery, dark green leaves and small white flowers in summer, 20 x 90cm (8 x 36in), 'Minor' is a smaller, more compact form with tiny leaves, ideal for a trough; *H. epacridea* prostrate mat with conifer-like leaves and scented white flowers, 45 x 60cm (18 x 24in); *H. pinguifolia* 'Pagei' AGM prostrate, rather loose mat with silver-grey foliage and white flowers in spring, in good growing conditions makes fine ground cover, 20 x 60cm (8 x 24in); *H. rigidula* erect much-branched shrub with leathery green leaves with grey undersides and white flowers, 30 x 30cm (12 x 12in).

Helianthemum
Rock rose

❝ Helianthemums are among those rather numerous plants that are equally at home in larger rock gardens and the front of borders. They are confused in some people's minds with Cistus *and both are sometimes called sun roses. This should tell you that, wherever you plant them, those bright flowers do need plenty of sunshine. ❞*

Origin Wide distribution in alpine meadows or open scrub in Europe, North and South America, Asia and northern Africa.
Habit Low, spreading evergreen sub-shrubs.
Flowering Season Early summer.
Size Most 20 x 30cm (8 x 12in), but some more vigorous at 30 x 45cm (12 x 18in).
Site Full sun and shelter from cold winds essential. Particularly successful on thin alkaline, dry soils.
Best Grown Outdoors, in a rock garden.

Features Small, often grey-green leaves with small, usually brightly coloured saucer-shaped flowers.
Special Care Protect from cold winds and trim back after flowering.
Propagation Take semi-ripe cuttings in summer. Species may be raised from seed sown in autumn.
Problems None.

Hebe pinguifolia 'Pagei'

Helianthemum 'Henfield Brilliant'

Hepatica

> ❝ Hepatica *is related to* Anemone; *this much is often stated. But it is therefore a member of the buttercup family Ranunculaceae and the similarity to buttercup flowers (if you forget about the colour) is striking but seldom remarked upon. They are excellent plants for the rock garden with more moist soil and, preferably, light shade.* ❞

Origin Northern temperate woodlands.
Habit Slow-growing herbaceous clumps.
Flowering Season Early spring.
Size 8–15 x 15–20cm (3–6 x 6–8in).
Site Partial shade and moist soil enriched with leaf mould.
Best Grown Outdoors, in a rock garden.

Features Kidney-shaped leaves and flowers like anemones, with coloured sepals and leafy bracts; these appear on wiry stems before the leaves.
Special Care Should not be disturbed once established, except to propagate.
Propagation Lift and divide mature plants in spring or sow ripe seed in late summer.
Problems Slugs, snails.

Hepatica nobilis

Hutchinsia
Chamois cress

❝ Chamois aren't simply the things that you use to polish your car. They begin life as part of a creature like a mountain goat that lives in some of the most inhospitable parts of Europe. And I assume that this little member of the brassica family has acquired its name because it similarly balances on cliffs and ledges. It is a pretty, moderately undistinguished but pleasant little alpine plant. ❞

Origin European mountains among limestone rocks and screes.
Habit Low, tufted evergreen perennial.
Flowering Season Late spring to early summer.
Size 5cm (2in) tall.
Site Sun or partial shade and fairly poor soil.
Best Grown Outdoors, on a scree, or in a trough or raised bed.

Features Pinnate foliage and four-petalled, cross-shaped flowers.
Special Care None.
Propagation Sow seed in spring or autumn, or remove self-sown seedlings from established plantings.
Problems None.

Recommended Varieties
Hutchinsia alpina (syn. *Thlaspi alpinum*) tiny plant with fern-like foliage and dense clusters of white flowers.

Hypericum

❝ Give a dog a bad name and hang him'. People have given Hypericum a bad name because H. calycinum is one of the most invasive and ineradicable of ground cover shrubs; the genus has been hanged in consequence. It's a great pity really, because tucked away among nearly 400 species are several much more modest and really rather attractive plants for the larger alpine garden. ❞

Hypericum balearicum

Origin Varies (see below).
Habit Varies, mostly evergreen or deciduous shrubs or herbaceous perennials.
Flowering Season Varies (see below).
Size 15–25 x 25–40cm (6–10 x 10–16in).
Site Sunny, open position and most soils, the less hardy types in well-drained conditions.
Best Grown Outdoors, in a rock garden.

Features Characteristically showy yellow flowers with noticeable stamens.
Special Care Protect from excessive winter wet.
Propagation Sow seed in spring or take semi-ripe cuttings of shrubby types in late summer.
Problems None.

Recommended Varieties
Hypericum balearicum barely hardy species from the Balearic Islands and Spain that requires protection in cold gardens, a low but dense evergreen shrub flowering from early to late summer, the leathery leaves are dark green and have wart-like growths on them, 25 x 25cm (10 x 10in); *H. cerastioides* (syn. *H. rhodoppeum*) hardy sub-shrub from south-eastern Europe with a semi-prostrate habit and downy grey-green foliage, a mass of flowers appears above the foliage from late spring to early summer, 15 x 40cm (6 x 16in); *H. coris* small plant with heath-like stems and pyramidal panicles of flowers that appear in early to midsummer, native of southern Europe that is barely hardy, tolerating down to -5°C (23°F), so propagate from semi-ripe cuttings in summer and grow in a warm site, 20 x 30cm (8 x 12in); *H. olympicum* AGM herbaceous with a woody base but often described as a deciduous shrub, the plant is covered with black glands and has grey-green foliage and abundant large summer flowers, hardy, probably the best of the group, from south-eastern Europe and western Asia, 25 x 30cm (10 x 12in).

Iberis Candytuft

" *Candytuft is one of those plants that turns up in almost everyone's list of subjects for a child's first garden. The reason is that it grows quickly with almost no attention. The candytuft concerned is the annual* Iberis amara, *but it has a number of perennial relatives, similarly pretty, similarly appealing – and perhaps good subjects for a child's first alpine garden.* "

Origin Widespread distribution, although most of those recommended below are from southern Europe, in open sites on alkaline soils.
Habit Evergreen sub-shrubs or perennials.
Flowering Season Varies (see below).
Size 25–30 x 40–60cm (10–12 x 16–24in).
Site Sunny, open site and neutral or alkaline soil preferred.
Best Grown Outdoors, in a rock garden.

Jovibarba sobolifera

Features Pretty four-petalled flowers: two long and two short.
Special Care Trim lightly after flowering.
Propagation Take softwood cuttings in late spring.
Problems Slugs, snails, caterpillars.

Recommended Varieties
Iberis gibraltarica evergreen sub-shrub with flat flowerheads of white to red-lilac, 30 x 60cm (12 x 24in); *I. semperflorens* evergreen sub-shrub from southern Italy, barely hardy, tolerating down to -5°C (23°F), forms a spreading mat of scented white flowers from winter to early spring, 30 x 60cm, 12 x 24in); *I. sempervirens* (syn. *I. commutata*) hardy, spreading evergreen sub-shrub from southern Europe, small white flowers, often tinted with lilac, appear from late spring to early summer, 30 x 40cm (12 x 16in), 'Schneeflocke' (syn. 'Snowflake') AGM mound-like habit and dense cover of pure white flowers, 25 x 60cm (10 x 24in).

Jovibarba

" *Jovibarba is a relatively new name to appear in gardening books although the genus has existed for a long time. What has happened is that recently a number of species that were more familiarly known as sempervivums have been moved there. They have a valuable role to play, because not very many plants with truly succulent foliage are hardy enough to be used in alpine gardening.* "

Origin Mountains of central and southern Europe, western Asia.
Habit Succulent perennials.
Flowering Season Summer.
Size 15 x 30cm (6 x 12in).
Site Full sun essential, thriving in poor soil or stony, gritty places and very drought tolerant. Those recommended are lime intolerant, others are not.
Best Grown Outdoors, in a scree bed, crevices or a trough. Alternatively, may also be grown in an alpine house.

Features Like houseleeks, they have fleshy leaves in rosettes but differ from houseleeks in their bell-shaped flowers.
Special Care The rosettes die off after flowering and should then be removed.
Propagation Remove offsets in spring or summer.
Problems None.

Recommended Varieties
The following species are mainly from the Alps and are not easily distinguished: *Jovibarba allionii* (syn. *J. hirta* subsp. *allionii*) leaf rosettes yellow-green and hairy with red tips, pale yellow-brown bell-shaped flowers in summer; *J. arenaria* (syn. *Sempervivum arenarium*) bright green leaf rosettes with pale green-yellow flowers; *J. sobolifera* (syn. *Sempervivum soboliferum*; hen and chickens houseleek) glossy bright green leaf rosettes with red tips, green-yellow flowers.

Lamium Deadnettle

" The sprawling little red-flowered deadnettle is one of the commonest annual weeds of the vegetable garden. I don't suggest that you grow it in your alpine bed, although in truth it is one of those plants that, if someone said this is a rare endemic from Szechuan, folk would pay good money for it. Its perennial relatives aren't rare either, but they do make a pretty if slightly untidy contribution to the alpine arena. "

Origin Europe, Asia, northern Africa.
Habit Carpeting semi-evergreen and evergreen perennials.
Flowering Season Late spring to early summer.
Size Varies (see below).
Site Best in partial shade but can tolerate sun, although foliage colour is less intense. Good choice for a poor, dry site.
Best Grown Outdoors, in a rock garden or large trough.

Lamium maculatum 'Aureum'

Features Angular, square stems, pairs of opposite leaves and two-lipped flowers.
Special Care Any unkempt foliage should be trimmed back hard after flowering.
Propagation Lift and divide plants in autumn or spring. Sow seed in spring or take stem-tip cuttings in summer.
Problems Leaf-eating beetles, mildew.

Recommended Varieties
Lamium garganicum subsp. *striatum* only 10cm (4in) high, not to be confused with the normal taller species, best in a sunny position; *L. maculatum* rhizomatous perennial that may be invasive, aromatic green leaves have a central white stripe and flowers are red or purple, 15–30 x 1m (6–12in x 3ft), 'Aureum' gold leaves with a white stripe, pink flowers, 'Roseum' (syn. 'Shell Pink') white-striped leaves, pale pink flowers; *L. orvala* (balm-leaved archangel) clump forming, leaves are rather coarse but the pink to dark purple flowers are impressive, 60 x 30cm (24 x 12in).

Lathyrus

" Lathyrus isn't that familiar a name simply because gardeners are more used to calling its species by the English name 'sweet pea'. The classic garden sweet pea is an annual, although there are perennial forms of it, too. The species I recommend here are also perennial but very much smaller, although still with that classically lovely flower form. "

Origin European woodlands.
Habit Tufted herbaceous perennials.
Flowering Season Late spring to early summer.
Size 20–45 x 45cm (8–18 x 18in).
Site Sun or partial shade, tolerant of most soils.
Best Grown Outdoors, in a rock garden.

Features Relative of the sweet pea with angular stems, pinnate leaves without tendrils and flowers similar to those of the sweet pea.
Special Care None.
Propagation Sow seed in spring.
Problems Aphids, slugs, snails, thrips.

Lathyrus cyaneus

Recommended Varieties
Lathyrus cyaneus species from the Caucasus that has bright blue flowers, but in other respects is similar to the more widely grown *L. vernus*; *L. vernus* (syn. *Orobus vernus*; spring vetchling) AGM flowers variable from blue-violet, through red-purple to pink.

Ledum Labrador tea

" *There are only a few species (some people say only one) of these cold-climate members of the heather family, and I assume they gained their common name because people in Labrador use the plant to produce a beverage. I think there are probably better ingredients for tea, but if you have a moist, acidic soil it is an interesting species to include in your alpine garden.* "

Origin Native to northern America and western Greenland, but naturalized in parts of Europe including Britain.
Habit Aromatic evergreen shrub.
Flowering Season Mid-spring to early summer.
Size The species is 90 x 120cm (3 x 4ft), but the compact form recommended below is much neater at only 30cm (12in) tall.
Site Partial shade and acidic soil that is cool and moist.
Best Grown Outdoors, in an acidic-soil bed or a heather garden.

Features Dense clusters of five-petalled flowers.
Special Care None.
Propagation Take semi-ripe cuttings in summer.
Problems None.

Recommended Varieties
Ledum groenlandicum 'Compactum' compact form of the species with woolly stems and white flowers.

Leontopodium Edelweiss

" *If ever a plant owed its success and familiarity to a song, this is it. I find it a rather ugly thing and not really a very easy plant to grow. That dense woolly, shaggy covering is extremely prone to attracting moisture, retaining it and then rotting in consequence.* "

Origin Mountains of southern Europe.
Habit Evergreen perennial.
Flowering Season Late spring to early summer.
Size 20 x 10cm (8 x 4in).
Site Full sun and well-drained soil that is neutral or alkaline.
Best Grown Outdoors in a raised bed, but better in an alpine house where it looks neater and less ragged.

Special Care None.
Propagation Sow ripe seed, or lift and divide plants in spring.
Problems Outdoors, slugs and snails; in an alpine house, also aphids and red spider mites.

Recommended Varieties
Leontopodium alpinum clump-forming perennial with grey-green leaves and yellow-white flowers surrounded by grey-white bracts, habit is variable from leggy to rather neat so choose plants carefully when buying, 'Mignon' selected form with a neater habit.

Features Simple hairy leaves and small, clustered flowerheads surrounded by a ruff of woolly bracts.

Leontopodium alpinum

PERENNIALS AND SHRUBS

Leptinella

❝ I am sure that some people are put off this very pretty plant by the fact that the most frequently seen species is called squalida. *It isn't alone in this, of course, and there are other 'squalid' plants. The name means, well, squalid, dingy or untidy, and simply serves to show what a disservice can be done to a species through an unthinking description by the person who gave it its name. ❞*

Origin Australia, New Zealand, South America.
Habit Carpeting semi-evergreen or evergreen perennials.
Flowering Season Varies with species, but within the range late spring to midsummer.
Size 15cm (6in) x more or less indefinite.
Site Sun or partial shade and fairly poor soil.
Best Grown Outdoors, in a rock garden or trough. Also makes useful ground cover and can withstand some trampling, so ideal for softening paving or for gravel gardens. *L. atrata* is sometimes grown in an alpine house.

Features Aromatic foliage and button-like flowerheads.
Special Care None.
Propagation Lift and divide plants in spring, or sow ripe seed in a cold frame.
Problems None, but some forms are invasive.

Leptinella squalida

Recommended Varieties
Leptinella atrata (syn. *Cotula atrata*) creeping perennial with fern-like grey-green foliage, stems have a purple tint, unusual rather than attractive purple-black flowerheads appear in late spring to early summer; *L. potentillina* (syn. *Cotula potentillina*) creeping stems that root at the nodes where the leaves (similar to those of a potentilla) are clustered together, purple flowerheads appear in early to midsummer; *L. squalida* (syn. *Cotula squalida*) slow-growing mat with a spread of up to 40cm (16in), purple flowers appear in midsummer.

Lewisia

❝ Let's begin at the beginning: I don't like lewisias. My opinion is dictated almost entirely because some of them have pink, orange and red colours that are best described as luminous. They are also troublesome little things, preferring to lie on their sides than to grow upright like proper plants, but huge numbers of alpine gardeners love them nonetheless. ❞

Lewisia Cotyledon Hybrid

Origin Western North America.
Habit Rosette-forming perennials, some evergreen, others dying down after flowering.
Flowering Season Varies, but most between spring and summer.
Size Varies, from dwarf forms at 10 x 10cm (4 x 4in) to larger types around 30 x 40cm (12 x 16in).
Site Full sun essential, soil neutral or acidic and very well drained or gritty.
Best Grown In pans in an alpine house. Some may be grown outside in a trough or wall.

Features Basal rosettes of leaves that vary in shape but are always fleshy, and funnel-shaped flowers.
Special Care A collar of fine grit will help prevent the plants from rotting in winter, although a popular alternative is to plant them on their sides in wall crevices. Plants grown on the flat outdoors will need winter protection in the form of a sheet of glass or a cloche.
Propagation Sow seed in autumn and keep in a cold frame over winter. Remove offsets from evergreen species in early summer.
Problems Outdoors, neck rot, slugs, snails; in an alpine house, aphids.

Recommended Varieties

Lewisia columbiana neat evergreen rosettes of narrow green leaves and small magenta flowers, 15 x 15cm (6 x 6in); *L. cotyledon* AGM evergreen Californian species that is one of the easiest to grow, flowers very showy and usually in shades of pink, but many strains are now available including f. *alba* with white flowers, 30 x 25cm (12 x 10in); Cotyledon Hybrids are clump-forming evergreen perennials derived from *L. cotyledon* with flowers in a wide range of bright colours including pink, magenta, yellow and orange, 15–30 x 20–40cm (6–12 x 8–16in); *L.* 'George Henley' showy cultivar like *L. columbiana* but with shorter, more compact flowers in purple-pink with magenta veins, 10 x 10cm (4 x 4in); *L. nevadensis* small deciduous type, white flowers in spring nestle among the leaves, very prone to damage through overwatering, 10 x 10cm (4 x 4in); *L.* 'Pinkie' deciduous dwarf hybrid with large pink flowers, 10 x 10cm (4 x 4in); *L. pygmaea* similar to *L. nevadensis* but with prostrate flowering stems bearing one or more white or pale pink flowers, 10 x 10cm (4 x 4in); *L. rediviva* (bitter-root) deciduous species that dies down very soon after flowering in summer and is best in an alpine house, 25 x 10cm (10 x 4in); *L. tweedyi* AGM another species that really requires an alpine house, beautiful evergreen with large fleshy leaves and large flowers in spring in a range of shades of peach and apricot, 20 x 30cm (10 x 12in).

Limnanthes
Poached egg plant

❝ *Undeniably a descriptive name, at least if you have seen the flowers, but scarcely flattering. Certainly if you grow* Limnanthes, *you can't complain at lack of floral interest, and, while I'm not sure if it is has a special attractiveness to insects, organic gardeners have taken it to their hearts for its value in luring beneficial insects to the garden.* ❞

Origin California.
Habit Erect or spreading hardy annual.
Flowering Season Late spring to midsummer.
Size 15–25 x 15–25cm (6–10 x 6–10in).
Site Full sun and moist but well-drained soil.
Best Grown Outdoors, in a rock garden or as a path edging.

Features Shallow, showy cup-shaped flowers.
Special Care None.
Propagation Sow seed in autumn, or in spring *in situ*.
Problems None, but may be invasive through self-seeding.

Recommended Varieties
Limnanthes douglasii AGM fern-like foliage, nectar-rich white flowers with yellow centres that are popular with bees and hoverflies, so widely used by organic gardeners to attract beneficial insects.

Linaria Toadflax

❝ *Nothing whatever to do with toads, although a fair bit to do with dragons: the flowers are like miniature snapdragons and very pretty, too. These are easy-to-grow plants that should be in all alpine gardens, and, if you fancy trying your hand at creating an alpine meadow, they will be indispensable.* ❞

Origin Mountains of central and southern Europe, on rocky slopes and screes.
Habit Herbaceous perennials.
Flowering Season Summer.
Size *L. alpina* 8 x 15cm (3 x 6in), *L. pyrenaica* 20 x 10cm (8 x 4in).
Site Full sun and best in poorer soils.
Best Grown Outdoors, in a rock garden, scree or wall crevice.

Features Narrow leaves and two-lipped flowers reminiscent of small snapdragons (*Antirrhinum*).
Special Care None.
Propagation Sow seed in autumn.
Problems Aphids, powdery mildew.

Recommended Varieties
Linaria alpina (alpine toadflax) trailing stems with blue-green leaves, violet and yellow flowers throughout the summer, short-lived perennial that self-seeds freely and can on occasion be invasive; *L. supina* variable perennial with narrow grey-green leaves on upright branches, flowers usually yellow but sometimes violet.

Linnaea Twin flower

" *How many botanists and horti-culturists pass this plant without according it the reverence to which it is due? Probably the vast major-ity, who will appreciate its bell-shaped flowers borne in pairs, but will not appreciate that this modest bit of botany is the only plant genus named in honour of the man who himself named more living things than anyone before or since: Linnaeus.* "

Linnaea borealis

Features Neat foliage and bell-shaped flowers.
Special Care None.
Propagation Take softwood cuttings in early summer, or remove rooted sections of stem between autumn and spring. Sow seed outdoors in autumn.
Problems None.

Origin Woodlands and heaths in North America and northern Eurasia.
Habit Prostrate evergreen shrub.
Flowering Season Summer.
Size *L. borealis* 8cm x 1m (3in x 3ft), var. *americana* 10 x 30cm (4 x 12in).
Site Partial shade or shade; acidic, moist, humus-rich soil essential.
Best Grown Outdoors, in a large rock garden or acidic-soil bed.

Recommended Varieties
Linnaea borealis tangled mat of glossy leaves with lightly scented, bell-shaped flowers in pale pink held well above it, var. *americana* North American form that is a little taller than the species and has deep pink flowers.

Linum Flax

" *Once or twice every year, someone asks me the name of the blue-flowered crop that has suddenly appeared in a farm field in their neighbourhood and which they have never seen before. The crop is flax, an ancient one that has seen some-thing of a comeback in recent times, although it is now being grown as a source of linseed rather than fibre. There are many species, however, in addition to the crop plant* Linum usitatissimum, *and several make excellent alpine garden subjects.* "

Features Slender stems and five-petalled flowers.

Special Care May need protection from winter wet.
Propagation Sow seed in autumn or take semi-ripe cuttings in summer.
Problems Slugs.

Origin Europe, Asia.
Habit Perennial tufts.
Flowering Season Summer.
Size Most within the range 20–30 x 20–30cm (8–12 x 8–12in).
Site Sun and light, fairly poor soil.
Best Grown Outdoors, in a rock garden or trough.

Recommended Varieties
Linum arboreum AGM dwarf ever-green shrub with thick blue-green leaves and large golden-yellow flow-ers, Mediterranean species that is only barely hardy, tolerating down to –5°C (23°F), 20–30 x 20–30cm (8–12 x 8–12in); *L. flavum* (golden flax) variable upright, woody peren-nial with dark green leaves and golden yellow flowers that open in the sun, 30 x 20cm (12 x 8in); *L.* 'Gemmell's Hybrid' AGM one of the best, being more compact than *L. arboreum* and covered in flowers but barely hardy, 15 x 20cm (6 x 8in); *L. monogynum* New Zealand species with a tuft of stems and lots of white flowers but barely hardy, taller than reaching average 45 x 30cm (18 x 12in); *L. narbonense* short-lived perennial forming a clump of wiry stems, covered in blue flowers in summer, each bloom lasts a day but there is a succession for many weeks, only barely hardy, 30–60 x 45cm (12–24 x 18in).

Lithospermum

❝ Lithospermums have very hard seeds; that's what the name Lithospermum *means. They are not, however, hard to grow, although many people seem to have difficulties with them. I think the problems in growing them successfully may lie in not paying enough attention to their site requirements. ❞*

Origin Southern Europe.
Habit Low evergreen shrub.
Flowering Season Late spring to early summer.
Size 20 x 60cm (8 x 24in).
Site Open, sunny and sheltered position; soil should be acidic or neutral and enriched with peat.
Best Grown Outdoors, in a rock garden, scree or large trough, or in an alpine house.

Features Hairy leaves and stemless, funnel-shaped flowers.
Special Care None.
Propagation Take semi-ripe cuttings in midsummer.
Problems In an alpine house, aphids and red spider mite.

Lithospermum diffusum 'Star'

Recommended Varieties
Lithospermum diffusum (syn. *Lithodora diffusa*) evergreen mat of woody stems with flowers in a rich gentian-blue.

Loiseleuria Alpine azalea, creeping azalea

❝ Loiseleuria *is the alpine equivalent of rhododendrons and azaleas. There is only one species, a common little inhabitant of arctic regions throughout the northern hemisphere, and it makes a very acceptable substitute for its grander, more familiar and much more numerous relatives further south. ❞*

Features Small leathery leaves and small bell-shaped flowers.
Special Care Does not flower well in dry areas.

Loiseleuria procumbens

Propagation Take softwood cuttings in early summer or semi-ripe cuttings in late summer. May also be layered in spring.
Problems None.

Origin High-lying or sub-arctic areas of North America, Europe and Asia.
Habit Dwarf, prostrate evergreen shrub.
Flowering Season Early summer.
Size 8 x 30cm (3 x 12in).
Site Full sun and acidic soil that is moist but well drained.
Best Grown Outdoors, in a rock garden or acidic-soil bed, or in an alpine house.

Recommended Varieties
Loiseleuria procumbens tight mat of glossy green leaves and small pink flowers in early summer.

Lychnis

❝ *Some species of* Lychnis *are called catchflies, a reference to their sticky glandular hairs on which many a fly has met a glutinous end. The flowers don't seem to be big enough for the foliage, but they are pretty little things nonetheless.* ❞

Origin Northern temperate and arctic regions.
Habit Evergreen or semi-evergreen perennials with opposite leaves, that sometimes form basal tufts.
Flowering Season Summer.
Size Varies, but within the range 15–35 x 15–45cm (6–14 x 6–18in).
Site Sun; tolerant of most types of soil.
Best Grown Outdoors, in a rock garden.

Recommended Varieties
Lychnis alpina (alpine campion, alpine catchfly) European species with a tuft of dark green leaves and head of pink-purple flowers, 15 x 15cm (6 x 6in); *L. x arkwrightii* hybrid between *L. x haageana* and *L. chalcedonica*, erect stems with attractive purple-brown leaves and loose heads of scarlet flowers from early to late summer, 35 x 35cm (14 x 14in), 'Vesuvius' has larger flowers in vivid scarlet; *L. flos-jovis* 'Nana' (syn. 'Minor') compact form of a variable species, with oval leaves covered in silver-white wool and red flowers, 25 x 45cm (10 x 18in).

Features The pretty flowers are formed of five petals, which are often notched.
Special Care None.
Propagation Lift and divide plants or take basal cuttings, both in spring. *L. x arkwrightii* may be raised from seed sown in autumn.
Problems Slugs.

Lychnis arkwrightii **'Molten Lava'**

Lysimachia
Creeping Jenny

❝ *Quite why it should be Jenny that creeps, I am unsure, but the 'creeping' epithet is appropriate to distinguish this lovely little species from some of the other members of the genus which are tall border perennials. It is a plant that I always delight in finding in the wild, and, although its native form has foliage of a bright yellow-green, the selected variant 'Aurea' is truly striking.* ❞

Origin Europe.
Habit Prostrate evergreen mat.
Flowering Season Early summer.
Size 5 x 40cm (2 x 16in), but spread indefinite if not controlled.
Site Sun or shade and most moist but well-drained soils.
Best Grown Outdoors, in a rock garden or trough.

Lysimachia nummularia **'Aurea'**

Features Long stems with round leaves and sparse, cup-shaped flowers.
Special Care Do not let the soil dry out in summer. May be invasive, so best cut back after flowering.
Propagation Remove naturally rooted creeping stems in late spring, lift and divide plants in autumn or spring, or sow seed in spring.
Problems None.

Recommended Varieties

Lysimachia nummularia (creeping Jenny) prostrate carpet of bright green leaves, sparse yellow flowers, 'Aurea' AGM gold-leaved variant that requires sun to maintain the leaf colour.

Maianthemum May lily

" May lilies do not only flower in May. In my garden, they start before and continue after; nor are they lilies, any more than their close relatives lilies-of-the-valley are lilies. They also share the attribute of an invasive tendency, but are good plants for a slightly shaded, large, semi-wild rock garden. These are not plants for a confined space. "

Features Heart-shaped leaves and clusters of small flowers.
Special Care None.
Propagation Lift and divide plants in spring, or sow ripe seed in autumn and keep in a cold frame over winter. Rooted runners may be separated in spring.
Problems Slugs, snails.

Origin Woodlands of the temperate northern hemisphere.
Habit Evergreen carpeting perennial.
Flowering Season Early summer.
Size 15cm (6in) x indefinite.
Site Partial shade or shade, and acidic or neutral soil that is moist and humus rich but well drained.
Best Grown Outdoors, making good ground cover.

Recommended Varieties

Maianthemum bifolium (false lily-of-the-valley) rhizomatous perennial with glossy, dark green leaves and fluffy white flowers in early summer, followed by small red fruits.

Matthiola Stock

" Stocks are yet another group of unspectacular, pretty but easy-to-grow ornamental members of the brassica family. But they are also one of the groups where size matters. Choose the wrong stock for your garden and you will create a totally unexpected effect. "

Origin Southern Europe.
Habit Woody perennial.
Flowering Season Late spring to midsummer.
Size 40–60 x 20cm (16–24 x 8in).
Site Sunny, sheltered and moist but well-drained soil.
Best Grown Outdoors, in a rock garden.

Matthiola fruticosa

Features Upright spikes of flowers.
Special Care Tends to be short lived.
Propagation Sow seed in autumn.
Problems None.

Recommended Varieties

Matthiola fruticulosa dwarf, hairy perennial with grey-green leaves and flowers that vary from yellow-brown to purple-red.

PERENNIALS AND SHRUBS

Mentha Mint

❝ *Working on the basis that you really shouldn't have anything invasive in a small rock garden, why does one of my smaller rock garden plantings contain a species of mint? The reason is because it is such a tiny thing that even its invasiveness is on a small scale. This plant must have the smallest flowers and leaves of almost any European plant and, while it does creep over the ground, the effect is to produce a little velvet carpet rather than anything problematic.* ❞

Features Minute aromatic leaves and tiny flowers.
Special Care Lift and divide every three years to keep plants healthy, and maintain soil moisture as they are intolerant of dry soil.

Origin Corsica, Sardinia, Monte Cristo.
Habit Semi-evergreen aromatic mat.
Flowering Season Early to mid-summer.
Size 1cm (½in) x indefinite.
Site Partial shade and damp soil.
Best Grown Outdoors, in cracks in paving or rocks, or alongside paths.

Recommended Varieties
Mentha requienii (syn. *M. corsica*; Corsican mint) mat of creeping stems, bright green leaves with intense peppermint aroma, tiny lilac flowers.

Mentha requienii

Propagation Lift and divide plants in spring.
Problems None.

Mertensia

❝ *The borage family is one of the more instantly recognizable for its individually rather lovely electric-blue or blue and red flowers and its extremely coarse, rather ugly foliage. Most are rather big, cumbersome plants, but at least one of those I recommend here is more in proportion with what you might expect from a rock garden species.* ❞

Features Attractive funnel- or bell-shaped flowers.
Special Care May be short lived, but easily propagated.
Propagation Lift and divide plants in spring, or sow ripe seed in autumn.
Problems Slugs, snails.

Origin North America, Greenland, northern Europe.
Habit Clump-forming or mat-like herbaceous perennials.
Flowering Season *M. maritima* summer, *M. pulmonarioides* mid- to late spring.
Size *M. maritima* 10 x 30cm (4 x 12in), *M. pulmonarioides* 45 x 25cm (18 x 10in).
Site Sun, but ideally with some shade at midday, and humus-rich, moist, reasonably fertile soil. *M. maritima* does best in sandy soil low in nutrients.
Best Grown Outdoors, in a rock garden.

Recommended Varieties
Mertensia maritima (oyster plant) spreading mat of slightly fleshy blue-green leaves, pink buds open to turquoise flowers in summer; *M. pulmonarioides* (syn. *M. virginica*; blue bells, Virginia cowslip) AGM a clump of blue-green leaves, in spring pink-mauve buds open to sky-blue or white flowers.

Myosotis Forget-me-not

❝ *The forget-me-nots are among the best loved of native and cottage garden flowers. They belong to the borage family and, as with others of the group, the foliage is at best rather coarsely hairy. But those tiny little flowers seem to entrance everyone and folk seem willing to forgive it all its other vices.* ❞

Myosotis alpestris

Origin *M. alpestris* Europe, *M. australis* New Zealand.
Habit Clump or mat-forming herbaceous perennials.
Flowering Season *M. alpestris* spring to early summer, *M. australis* early to midsummer.
Size 20 x 15cm (8 x 6in).
Site Sun or partial shade and moist but well-drained soil.
Best Grown Outdoors, in a rock garden, or in an alpine house.

Features Hairy leaves and dainty flowers.
Special Care None.
Propagation Sow seed in spring in a cold frame.
Problems Slugs, snails, powdery mildew, downy mildew.

Recommended Varieties
Myosotis alpestris (*M. rupicola*; alpine forget-me-not) found in damp woods and mountain meadows, short-lived plant producing clumps of bright green foliage and bright blue flowers with a yellow eye; *M. australis* erect and hairy species with white or yellow flowers.

Omphalodes Navelwort

❝ *It seems impossible to escape the Boraginaceae on these pages, as here is another. But this is a plant that has always seemed to me to possess the virtues of forget-me-nots, without those vices. The foliage is evergreen, although liable to be a bit frayed and browned in cold weather; but, in the flowers, borage family blue was never bluer.* ❞

Origin Europe, Asia.
Habit Herbaceous, almost evergreen perennials and reliably so in mild winters.
Flowering Season Spring.
Size *O. cappadocica* 25 x 30–45cm, (10 x 12–18in), *O. luciliae* 10 x 15cm (4 x 6in), *O. verna* 20 x 30cm (8 x 12in).
Site Partial shade, although some can tolerate sun; cool, fairly moist, humus-rich soil is preferred, but worth trying on drier sites if organic matter is added.
Best Grown Outdoors, in a rock garden, although *O. luciliae* is better in an alpine house.

Features Grown for their forget-me-not-like flowers.
Special Care Carefully cut away any frayed and browned foliage in early spring.
Propagation Lift and divide plants in spring. Sow seed in spring or take basal cuttings in early summer.
Problems None.

Omphalodes cappadocica

Recommended Varieties
Omphalodes cappadocica AGM easy-to-grow species from the woodlands of the Caucasus, dense spreading clumps of glossy, oval green leaves and branching sprays of electric-blue flowers in spring, much the best coloured form, 'Cherry Ingram' is a more compact variety with larger flowers in deep blue; *O. luciliae* species that inhabits limestone rock crevices in mountains of Greece and western Asia, a loose tuft of semi-evergreen blue-grey leaves, the early flowers are pink but then turn a light sky-blue, an interesting flower colour that is an acquired taste but not an easy plant to grow well; *O. verna* (blue-eyed Mary, creeping forget-me-not), European species from the Alps with heart-shaped leaves and a trailing habit, spreads by runners and needs to be sited with care as may be invasive, flowers are blue with a white throat and appear from early to late spring, best in a shady position and acidic soil, 'Alba' has pure white flowers.

PERENNIALS AND SHRUBS

Oxalis

❝ *One of the first tasks I undertake when checking a new piece of land for its gardening suitability is to see if there are any clump-forming plants with trifoliate leaves and bright pink flowers. Yes, there's no doubt that the all-but-ineradicable pink-flowered species of* Oxalis *have given the genus a notorious reputation. But it also includes the first alpine plant I ever bought and one that I have grown and loved throughout the years since.* ❞

Features Some have trefoil leaves and flax-like flowers that open in sun.
Special Care None, but be aware that some other species are extremely invasive.
Propagation Sow seed in warmth in late winter or early spring. Lift and divide plants in spring or detach offsets.
Problems Slugs, snails, rust.

Origin Widespread, but those recommended below are from South America or southern Africa.
Habit Many are clump-forming, bulbous perennials.
Flowering Season Varies, mostly summer.
Size Varies, but within the range 5–10 x 10–20cm (2–4 x 4–8in).
Site Sun or partial shade; best in slightly moist and fairly rich soil.
Best Grown Outdoors, in a raised bed or trough, although some are better in an alpine house.

Recommended Varieties

Oxalis adenophylla AGM South American species that makes an attractive clump both outdoors and in an alpine house, the fibrous bulbs lie on the surface of the soil and produce a tuft of grey leaves, funnel-shaped purple-pink flowers appear from mid- to late spring and the plants die down in autumn; *O. depressa* (syn. *O. inops*) species from southern Africa that is only barely hardy, tolerating down to -5°C (23°F), and requires full sun, can be invasive as it spreads by short runners, green trefoil leaves with dark spots and large rose-pink flowers with yellow centres make this a very striking plant; *O. lobata* attractive South American species that needs full sun and is only barely hardy, trefoil leaves of bright green and yellow flowers with light red veins, the leaves die away in early summer but new leaves appear with the flowers in late summer to early autumn; *O. obtusa* slow-growing, mat-like species from southern Africa with runners that produce bulbils, in summer it is covered with rose-pink flowers with yellow centres, only barely hardy.

Papaver Poppy

❝ *Much as I would like alpine poppies to be neat and compact versions of their tall, spindly border relatives, they really aren't. A small poppy is still a small poppy, with all of its bigger relatives' drawbacks. Their flowers have that papery charm, but the plant is a bit of a sprawling thing and, while this is acceptable in a large rock garden (and, best of all, a scree garden), it isn't in a small one. If you have or want to try an alpine meadow, however, this is a plant that you really must have.* ❞

Left: Oxalis adenophylla
Right: Papaver alpinum

Origin Mostly Europe and temperate Asia.
Habit Short-lived herbaceous perennials.
Flowering Season Summer.
Size 15–20 x 10cm (6–8 x 4in).
Site Full sun and very well-drained soil.
Best Grown Outdoors, in a rock garden.

Features Finely divided foliage and saucer-shaped flowers.
Special Care None.
Propagation Sow seed in spring or autumn. Plants hybridize readily to produce very mixed seedlings when self-sown.
Problems Aphids, fungal wilts, downy mildew.

Recommended Varieties
Papaver alpinum (alpine poppy) this name is used to cover many species native to the Alps and Pyrenees, short-lived perennials with finely divided, grey-green leaves and saucer-shaped flowers in orange, red, yellow or white, the latter forms sometimes called *P. burseri* (syn. *P. alpinum* subsp. *burseri*); *P. miyabeanum* compact Japanese alpine poppy, similar to *P. alpinum* but with yellow-green foliage and cream to pale yellow flowers; *P. sendtneri* tufted species from the Pyrenees with yellow or orange flowers and blue-green leaves.

Parahebe

Hebes are woody, evergreen veronicas, and parahebes differ from them very little, although all are more or less prostrate and ideally suited therefore to alpine gardens. Like hebes, they also originate in New Zealand, which means that, while some can withstand some fierce winters, most are generally less than fully hardy in Europe, although those I recommend here will tolerate the conditions in most of our gardens.

Origin New Zealand in sunny, dry, stony habitats.
Habit Semi-woody, evergreen or semi-evergreen shrubs.
Flowering Season Late summer to early autumn.
Size *P. catarractae* 30 x 30cm (12 x 12in), *P. lyallii* 25 x 50cm (10 x 20in).
Site Full sun in a sheltered position and fairly moist, moderately fertile soil.
Best Grown Outdoors, in a large rock garden, a gravel garden or at the edge of a raised bed.

Features Oval leaves and flowers like speedwells.

Special Care None.
Propagation Sow ripe seed and keep in a cold frame over winter. Take semi-ripe cuttings in summer and then protect them from winter wet.
Problems Slugs.

Recommended Varieties
P. catarractae AGM erect evergreen with purple young shoots and white flowers with a red eye and purple veins; *P. lyallii* semi-prostrate shrub whose low branches often root where they touch the ground, semi-evergreen with leathery foliage and white or pink flowers with purple veins.

67

PERENNIALS AND SHRUBS

Penstemon

❝ *Border penstemons are less than fully hardy in many areas and the dilemma is between leaving them in the ground over winter, leaving them in the ground with protection, lifting them, or growing them (as I do) in containers for taking under cover. Fortunately, the dwarf, alpine species are, in my experience, hardy enough in most districts.* ❞

Features Pretty two-lipped flowers rather like tiny snapdragons (*Antirrhinum*).
Special Care Dead-head faded flowers regularly. Plants tend to be short lived.

Propagation Sow seed in late winter or spring in a cold frame. Take semi-ripe cuttings in midsummer.
Problems Slugs, snails, powdery mildew.

> **Origin** North America, Mexico.
> **Habit** Herbaceous perennials or semi-shrubby evergreens.
> **Flowering Season** Mostly summer.
> **Size** Most 20–25 x 25–30cm (8–10 x 10–12in), but *P. rupicola* 10 x 45cm (4 x 18in).
> **Site** Full sun and a warm site, often better in fairly poor soil.
> **Best Grown** Outdoors, in a rock garden or large trough.

> **Recommended Varieties**
> *Penstemon fruticosus* var. *scouleri* (syn. *P. scouleri*) AGM erect evergreen sub-shrub producing a mass of flowers in late spring to early summer, but the colour varies from pale to deep purple, 30 x 30cm (12 x 12in); *P. laetus* var. *roezlii* similar to *P. newberryi* (below) but with a neater habit and clear cherry-red flowers, 20 x 25cm (8 x10in); *P. newberryi* AGM evergreen, mat-like sub-shrub with leathery dark green leaves and young stems covered with down, masses of bright pink-red flowers in midsummer, 25 x 30cm (10 x 12in), *P. pinifolius* AGM spreading evergreen sub-shrub with bright green, needle-like foliage and bright scarlet, tubular flowers in late summer, barely hardy, tolerating down to –5°C (23°F), 20 x 25cm (8 x 10in); *P. rupicola* (rock penstemon) AGM prostrate, evergreen sub-shrub with thick grey-green leaves and rose-carmine flowers in late spring to early summer, barely hardy.

Phlox

❝ *Forget about the big border* Phlox *when choosing alpine species, for the resemblance is minimal. There is something to be said for forgetting* Phlox *in its entirety, because I find them rather untidy, sprawling plants that soon take on a strawy appearance and are seldom truly neat. But they must be among the most widely bought alpine plants, so evidently many people are perfectly content with what they provide.* ❞

Features Masses of flowers in showy colours.
Special Care None.

> **Origin** North America.
> **Habit** Mat- or cushion-forming evergreen perennials.
> **Flowering Season** Mid- to late spring.
> **Size** 5–8 x 25cm (2–3 x 10in).
> **Site** Full sun and best in slightly poorer soils.
> **Best Grown** Outdoors, in a dry wall, or in an alpine house.

> **Recommended Varieties**
> *Phlox kelseyi* 'Rosette' dwarf cushion of slightly succulent leaves with clusters of deep violet-pink flowers, 5cm (2in) high; *P. subulata* (moss phlox) highly variable species but there are many varieties worth looking out for, habits vary but all flower from mid- to late spring.

***Phlox subulata* 'Amazing Grace'**

Propagation Take softwood cuttings in spring after flowering.
Problems None.

Phuopsis

6 *There's one part of my garden that is very much more smelly than any other. Strange to relate, it isn't the compost corner, which has a rather pleasantly organic fragrance. It is a corner of one of my alpine plantings, where* Phuopsis stylosa *imbues all around with an scent that suggests that a good many foxes have passed that way very recently. Yet this foxy odour really is a small price to pay for a rather good, if sprawling, ground cover plant for the bigger alpine planting.* 99

Origin Caucasus Mountains, north-eastern Iran.
Habit Low-growing, semi-evergreen perennial.
Flowering Season Late spring to early summer.
Size 15 x 50cm (6 x 20in).
Site Full sun or partial shade and moderately fertile, moist soil.
Best Grown Outdoors, in a rock garden or at the edge of paving.

Recommended Varieties
Phuopsis stylosa (syn. *Crucianella stylosa*) pale green leaves, pink tubular flowers, pungent smell of foxes that attracts butterflies, more or less evergreen in all except the coldest areas, 'Purpurea' has deeper purple-pink flowers.

Features Produces a carpet of tubular flowers.
Special Care Trim back after flowering to keep the plant neat.
Propagation Lift and divide plants in spring, or take semi-ripe cuttings in early summer. The species may be raised from seed sown in autumn.
Problems None.

Polygala Milkwort

6 *Milkwort was once believed to promote the flow of milk. I'm not sure that this is a claim to be taken too seriously, but it will certainly promote the flow of comments about its curiously bicoloured flowers. But be warned: don't fall in love with the rather charming little species called* Polygala chamaebuxus *unless you have an acidic soil.* 99

Origin *P. calcarea* western Europe including Britain, *P. chamaebuxus* Alps and Carpathians.
Habit Evergreen perennials or shrubs.
Flowering Season Late spring to early summer.
Size 5–15 x 20–30cm (2–6 x 8–12in).
Site *P. calcarea* requires sun and is longer lived in an alkaline soil; *P. chamaebuxus* requires sun or light shade and moist, lime-free soil.
Best Grown Outdoors, in a rock garden, or in an alpine house.

Features Usually leathery leaves, and small pea-like flowers.
Special Care None.

Phuopsis stylosa 'Purpurea'

Propagation Sow seed in autumn or take semi-ripe cuttings in late summer.
Problems Aphids and whitefly in an alpine house.

Recommended Varieties
Polygala calcarea prostrate, evergreen short-lived perennial with a basal rosette and trailing stems, deep blue flowers with white fringed lips; *P. chamaebuxus* (shrubby milkwort) AGM small, spreading evergreen shrub, the striking flowers have yellow lips, white or pale yellow wings and a yellow keel that ages to purple, var. *grandiflora* AGM has flowers with deep purple-pink wings and yellow lips.

Potentilla

❝ *Potentillas come in a considerable range of sizes, colours and, to some degree, shapes too. There are big, upright bushy things and low-growing sprawling, creeping things. They have the inestimable value of flowering over a very long period of the summer, but for your alpine plantings do check that your soil isn't too wet, and don't choose the big shrubbery varieties.* ❞

Potentilla aurea

Origin Widespread in the northern hemisphere.
Habit Evergreen sub-shrubs.
Flowering Season Mostly summer.
Size 8–20 x 15–30cm (3–8 x 6–12in).
Site Full sun and an open site, thriving on poor soils.
Best Grown Outdoors, in a rock garden.

Features Strawberry-like leaves (which betray their fairly close relationship to true strawberries) and saucer-shaped flowers.
Special Care None.
Propagation Sow seed in autumn or spring and keep in a cold frame. Lift and divide plants in autumn or spring, or take semi-ripe cuttings in summer.
Problems None.

Recommended Varieties

Potentilla aurea (golden cinquefoil) mat-forming plant from the Alps and Pyrenees, glossy green leaves with silky margins, the golden-yellow flowers often have orange centres and appear from late spring to summer, 'Plena' is a pretty double-flowered form; *P. crantzii* (alpine cinquefoil) similar to *P. aurea* but with more erect flower stems to 15cm (6in) and yellow flowers, the margins of the leaves are not silky, mountains of Europe, western Asia and northern America; *P. dubia* (syn. *P. brauniana*) small tufted plant with slightly hairy leaves and small yellow flowers, 8cm (3in) high, found in the Pyrenees and Alps on limestone rocks; *P. nitida* 'Rubra' low cushion or mat-like perennial with silver-hairy foliage, best planted in a rock crevice and prefers lime, large but sparse flowers in a rich rose-red appear from early to midsummer, from the southern Alps and Apennines; *P. x tonguei* AGM hybrid of garden origin between *P. anglica* or *P. aurea* and *P. nepalensis*, clump-forming plant with long, spreading stems and dark green, bronze-tinted leaves, the bowl-shaped, apricot-yellow flowers with crimson eyes appear from early summer to early autumn.

Pratia

❝ *Pratias are plants that I discovered relatively recently in my gardening career, and as each season goes by I am increasingly pleased that I did. They are good plants for paving, although they won't tolerate being completely flattened by trampling feet, and they are marvellous in a rock garden or very big trough.* ❞

Pratia pedunculata 'County Park'

Origin Australia.
Habit Creeping evergreen perennials.
Flowering Season Early summer to mid-autumn.
Size 3cm (1¼in) x indefinite.
Site Partial shade or shade and soil that is cool and moist.
Best Grown Outdoors, in an acidic-soil bed or a moist rock garden.

Features Small succulent leaves and lobelia-like flowers.
Special Care Dig in leaf mould to improve drier soils.
Propagation Lift and divide plants in spring.
Problems Slugs, snails. May be invasive in favourable conditions.

Recommended Varieties
Pratia pedunculata mat of pale green, thread-like stems, flowers are star shaped and very pale blue, 'County Park' has rich blue flowers that are almost stemless.

Pulsatilla Pasque flower

❝ *Pulsatillas are grand anemones, or grand buttercups if you prefer. Their feathery ruffs give them a wonderfully regal appearance, especially when combined with the deep violet flowers that some possess. But remember that the feathery ruff is not as good as real feathers at throwing off water and they will rot in very damp places.* ❞

Origin Alpine meadows in Europe and northern America.
Habit Herbaceous perennials.
Flowering Season Spring.
Size 10–30 x 10–20cm (4–12 x 4–8in).
Site Sun and humus-rich soil; *P. alpina* and *P. vulgaris* are best in alkaline soils.
Best Grown Outdoors, in a rock garden or scree, or in an alpine house.

Features Fern-like feathery foliage and silky anemone-like flowers.
Special Care All resent root disturbance and are best if protected from winter wet. The flowers are especially prone to damage from soil being splashed onto them, so a mulch of gravel or chips is important.

Recommended Varieties
Pulsatilla alpina (alpine pasque flower) clump-forming perennial from mountains of central and western Europe, with finely divided hairy foliage and cup-shaped flowers, white with a purple flush on the reverse, the petals are silky and there are prominent yellow stamens, can be reluctant to flower but if flowering is successful ornamental seedheads follow, subsp. *sulphurea* AGM thrives in acidic soil and has pale yellow flowers; *P. halleri* AGM tufted perennial from central and south-eastern Europe and the Crimea, similar to *P. vulgaris* but covered in silver hairs, bears bell-shaped flowers of a silky purple in late spring, subsp. *slavica* has less finely divided leaves and deep

Propagation Sow ripe seed and keep in a cold frame over winter, or take root cuttings in winter.
Problems Slugs, snails.

Pulsatilla alpina

purple flowers; *P. vernalis* (spring pasque flower) AGM clump-forming perennial from mountains of Spain, Scandinavia, Bulgaria and Russia with a cluster of light green leaves, the earliest to flower in mid-spring, bell-shaped flowers of silky white with a blue-violet flush and golden-yellow stamens, because they are so often damaged by the weather it is best grown in an alpine house; *P. vulgaris* (pasque flower) AGM from Britain and western France to the Ukraine, flowers are nodding at first then open to an erect star shape, variable species with many flower colours including purple, pink, mauve, red and white, among many named forms 'Eva Constance' has brick-red flowers and var. *rubra* deep red flowers.

Primula

❝ *This is one of the great genera of temperate-climate gardening.*
Primula *is a genus of huge diversity, much beauty, and much challenge.
Among around 425 species there are plants for every taste and every alpine
planting. But don't be too beguiled when you visit a specialist nursery. Do
check if your chosen plants require the protection of an alpine house, do
check if they are likely to be frustratingly short lived, and do check that
your soil requirements are exactly what is needed. Even among the five
beautiful British native species, there is a wide range of specific habitats to
be met if they are really to thrive well.* ❞

Origin Temperate zones of the
northern hemisphere.
Habit Herbaceous perennials, with
a basal rosette of leaves that is
sometimes evergreen.
Flowering Season Spring.
Size Varies, but most 15–30 x
20–30cm (6–12 x 8–12in), dwarf
types 7–10 x 10–20cm (2¾–4 x
4–8in).
Site Partial shade, although some
tolerate sun, especially if the soil is
moist.
Best Grown Outdoors, in a rock
garden, trough or scree, or in an
alpine house, depending on species.

Primula allionii **hybrid**

Features Tubular or bell-shaped flowers borne in a wide variety of heads.
Special Care Take care with watering; some varieties will rot if it collects
in the leaves. Some require winter protection.
Propagation Sow seed in autumn on
the surface of the compost and keep
cool. Lift and divide plants in summer
after flowering. A few, such as *Primula
allionii*, may be raised from basal cuttings taken in late spring.
Problems Aphids, red spider mite,
leafhopper, vine weevil, slugs, viruses,
primula brown core, grey mould.

Primula cockburniana

Recommended Varieties
There are several hundred species,
most suitable for one or other form
of alpine garden, so this is inevitably a
very small, very personal selection. A
few have a white meal called farina on
their foliage or other parts; this is a
highly prized feature, but usually indi-
cates that the plants will fare better in
an alpine house. *Primula allionii* cliffs of
western Europe and the maritime
Alps, low mound of sticky, grey-green
leaves covered in stemless flowers,
colour varies from pink to red-purple
or magenta-pink but all have a white
eye, best in an alpine house and is
lime tolerant, in addition to the
species there are a very large number
of good varieties, 7–10 x 20cm (2¾–4
x 8in); *P. aureata* evergreen species
from Nepal where it grows on moist
cliffs and rocky hillsides, requires an
alpine house and even then is difficult
to grow as it spends the winter as a
resting bud and during this time is
vulnerable to rot, nonetheless a very
desirable plant with toothed, very
white-mealy mid-green leaves and a
cluster of orange-yellow flowers with
a darker yellow eye, 8 x 20cm (3 x
8in); *P.* x *berninae* 'Windrush' hybrid
of garden origin with a small, neat
rosette of leaves and red-purple flowers with a white eye, 7 x 13cm (2¾ x
5in); *P.* x *bileckii* dwarf evergreen from
Austria with leathery, toothed leaves
and bright deep pink flowers with
white eyes in late spring, may be
grown in an alpine house or acidic-
soil bed, 7 x 10cm (2¾ x 4in); *P.
bracteosa* species from Bhutan with a
flat rosette of white-mealy, toothed

leaves and many-flowered cluster of pink-lilac flowers with toothed petals and a yellow eye surrounding a white halo, grow outdoors in a moist, shady position, 10 x 10cm (4 x 4in); *P. clarkei* miniature species from moist hillsides in Kashmir, it thrives in a moist peaty soil or compost either outdoors or in an alpine house, produces a small rosette of toothed pale green leaves and flat rose-pink flowers with a yellow eye, 7 x 15cm (2¾ x 6in); *P. clusiana* evergreen species from the Alps with dark leathery leaves, rose-pink to lilac flowers with a white eye appear in late spring, grow it in an alpine house or outdoors in a slightly alkaline soil, 8 x 15cm (3 x 6in); *P. cockburniana* small candelabra type from western China that is short lived but will self-seed if you are lucky, long slender stems bear orange-red flowers in late spring, requires moist soil in either sun or partial shade, 15 x 10cm (6 x 4in); *P. denticulata* (drumstick primula) AGM the mauve or purple spherical flowerheads are a familiar and welcome sight in spring, an easy-to-grow primula from China and the Himalayas that thrives in any moist soil in sun or partial shade, 40 x 20cm (16 x 8in); *P. elatior* (oxlip) AGM evergreen to semi-evergreen, rosette-forming perennial, similar to a cowslip but the flowers are usually held on one side, Europe and western Asia, 30 x 25cm (12 x 10in); *P. ellisiae* species found in moist rock crevices in New Mexico, forms a rosette of fairly large leaves up to 15cm (6in) long, from late spring to early summer there are flowers of pink-purple with a yellow eye, may be grown in an alpine house or

outdoors, 30 x 30cm (12 x 12in); *P. farinosa* (bird's eye primrose), a rosette of green leaves with white-mealy undersides, lilac-pink flowers with a yellow eye appear in spring, grow outdoors in sun or partial shade in an acidic humus-rich soil or in an alpine house, tends to be short lived, Europe and Asia, 25 x 25cm (10 x 10in); *P. halleri* similar growing conditions and appearance to *P. farinosa* but with a longer flower tube, the leaves have white-mealy undersides and the flowers are mauve-violet with a yellow eye; *P. integrifolia* one of the smallest European species from the Alps and Pyrenees, prostrate stems create a carpeting effect, a few rose to magenta flowers; *P. juliae* species from the Caucasus with creeping woody stems and deep red-purple flowers with a yellow eye, may be grown outside or in an alpine house, 7 x 25cm (2¾ x 10in); *P. marginata* AGM main features are the white-mealy foliage and stems, grow it in an alpine house or outside in full sun, flowers are variable from a clear blue to mauve-blue but there are numerous good named varieties offering more precise shades, 15 x 30cm (6 x 12in); *P. minima* tiny species found growing in alpine meadows, the pink or white flowers are large for the size of the plant but not prolific, petals are deeply notched forming a 'Y' shape, keep this plant moist for best results, 5cm high (2in); *P. nana* (syn. *P. edgeworthii*) Himalayan species, may be grown outside if protected from winter wet although generally best in an alpine house, white-mealy leaves and late-winter flowers that may be blue, lilac

or mauve with a yellow and white eye, 10 x 15cm (4 x 6in); *P. petiolaris* evergreen perennial from the Himalayas with pink, magenta or purple flowers with a yellow and white eye, either provide winter protection or grow in an alpine house, 10 x 20cm (4 x 8in); *P. x pubescens* AGM hybrid of garden origin between *P. auricula* and *P. hirsuta*, many named varieties exist offering different flower colours in shades of red, pink, purple or white, most with white-mealy foliage, 15 x 30cm (6 x 12in); *P. scotica* species from northern Scotland with dark red-purple flowers and a yellow eye, ideal in a pot or trough, 8 x 6cm (3 x 2½in); *P. veris* (cowslip) AGM much-loved British native but also found in Europe and Asia, heads of nodding, fragrant yellow flowers, 25 x 25cm (10 x 10in); *P. vulgaris* (primrose), very familiar British native woodland plant with fragrant pale yellow flowers, 20 x 35cm (8 x 14in); *P. whitei* species from the eastern Himalayas with pale to dark blue flowers with a white eye, 6 x 10cm (2½ x 4in).

Primula scotica

PERENNIALS AND SHRUBS

Pyrola Round-leaved wintergreen

  I've always assumed that Pyrola *is called wintergreen for the reason that evergreen ferns tend to be called wintergreen: they stay green in winter. Why these, of all evergreen plants, should be singled out in such a way is a bit of a mystery, but they have a certain charm.*

Origin Europe including Britain, North America.
Habit Creeping evergreen perennial.
Flowering Season Late spring to midsummer.
Size 20 x 15cm (8 x 6in).
Site Light to moderate shade; soil should be acidic and moist but well drained and fertile.
Best Grown Outdoors, in an acidic-soil bed or a rock garden.

Features Basal cluster of rounded leaves and upright stems of cup-shaped flowers with incurving petals.
Special Care Dig in leaf mould or chopped conifer needles if available. Avoid disturbing the roots.
Propagation Sow ripe seed on the surface of the compost in autumn. Lift and divide plants in spring.
Problems Slugs, snails.

Recommended Varieties
Pyrola rotundifolia evergreen perennial with lightly scented white flowers.

Ramonda

  No, you aren't seeing things. Ramondas do look very like their relative the African violet, but these charming little plants are European, not African, hardy and fully at home in any alpine collection. .

Origin *R. myconi* Pyrenees and north-eastern Spain, *R. nathaliae* Bosnia, Macedonia and northern Greece; both grow in shaded cliff crevices.
Habit Rosette-forming evergreen perennials.
Flowering Season Late spring to early summer.
Size 10 x 10–20cm (4 x 4–8in).
Site Partial shade and moist but well-drained soil.
Best Grown Outdoors, in an acidic-soil bed or rock garden, or in an alpine house.

Features Saucer-shaped flowers.
Special Care Plant on their sides, ideally in a shady wall crevice, to prevent water gathering in the leaf rosettes.
Propagation Sow ripe seed in autumn and keep in a cold frame; grow on for two years. Remove rosettes and plant in early summer, or take leaf cuttings in early autumn.
Problems Slugs, snails.

Ranunculus Mountain buttercup

  There's often a reluctance for gardeners to buy and plant species that belong to genera much better known as weeds. Ranunculus *comes into this category and the blooms of most species do indeed look like buttercups.*

Ramonda myconi

Recommended Varieties
Ramonda myconi (syn. *R. pyrenaica*) AGM looks rather like an African violet, to which it is distantly related, with dark green leaves that are crinkled and hairy and topped with blue-violet flowers with yellow stamens; *R. nathaliae* AGM similar species, but neater and with paler leaves that are more shiny and less rough.

Origin Temperate regions.
Habit Herbaceous perennials.
Flowering Season Mostly spring to early summer.
Size *R. crenatus* only 8 x 8cm (3 x 3in), but most are 20–45 x 30cm (8–18 x 12in).
Site Sun or partial shade and moist but well-drained soil, unless otherwise stated.
Best Grown Outdoors, in a rock garden or scree, or in an alpine house.

Recommended Varieties
Ranunculus amplexicaulis from the meadows of the Pyrenees, large white flowers in late spring to early summer, 30 x 20cm (12 x 8in); *R. calandrinioides* AGM species from the Atlas Mountains of Morocco, large poppy-like flowers that are white with a pink flush plus a centre of golden stamens, the foliage appears above ground in autumn and is an attractive feature being fleshy and a cool blue-green colour, the flowers appear in winter so it is ideally grown in an alpine house, the plant dies down in summer, 20 x 15cm (8 x 6in); *R. crenatus* tiny species with white flowers in early summer, found in Greece and Hungary in high alpine screes, 8 x 8cm (3 x 3in); *R. parnassiifolius* one of the best alpine buttercups with a basal rosette of dark green heart-shaped leaves, in early summer large white flowers with golden stamens appear, ageing to pink, buy them in flower as the species is variable, Alps and Pyrenees, 15 x10cm (6 x 4in).

Features Basal rosettes of often attractive foliage and five-petalled flowers.
Special Care Keep moist in summer, except for the tuberous species which should be allowed to dry out over the summer.

Propagation Sow ripe seed in autumn and keep in a cold frame; germination may be slow and erratic, and you will need to check that algae don't smother the compost.
Problems Aphids, powdery mildew, slugs, snails.

Raoulia Scabweed

6 *Raoulias have probably frustrated me more than any other alpine plants. It's not that they won't grow or establish: it's simply that they are so prone to dying off in the centre and turning a very pretty woolly carpet of growth into something resembling a tattered old rug. I'm sure that the secret is to give them more protection from winter wet, although this is not easy to achieve without unsightly cloches.* 99

Origin New Zealand.
Habit Cushion, hummock or mat of tiny evergreen leaves.
Flowering Season Flowers insignificant.
Size 1 x 20–30cm (½ x 8–12in).
Site Sun or partial shade in a warm, sheltered area and light, free-draining soil.
Best Grown Outdoors, in a scree or raised bed, or in an alpine house.

Recommended Varieties
Raoulia australis prostrate mat of silver foliage; *R. hookeri* similar but with pale green leaves; *R. tenuicaulis* the easiest to grow, with leaves covered in white wool.

Features Grown for their pretty, woolly foliage.
Special Care Only barely hardy, tolerating down to −5°C (23°F), so protect with a sheet of glass or a cloche in winter.
Propagation Remove already rooted tufts in spring.
Problems In an alpine house, aphids and red spider mite; outdoors, very prone to die off in the centre.

Raoulia australis

PERENNIALS AND SHRUBS

Rubus

❝ *Rubus is the genus that includes blackberries, raspberries and other things that are good to eat. But it's also by and large a genus of plants from cold places that may never be really beautiful en masse, although their flowers have an individual charm. Although not having quite the spreading potential of the common bramble, they are nevertheless plants for larger spaces rather than small rock gardens.* ❞

Origin R. *arcticus* arctic regions, R. *illecebrosus* Japan.
Habit Deciduous or semi-evergreen shrubs.
Flowering Season Early to mid-summer.
Size 15-30cm (6-12in) x indefinite.
Site Sun or partial shade and moderately fertile soil; best in moist conditions but will tolerate dryness.
Best Grown Outdoors, in a rock garden.

Recommended Varieties
Rubus arcticus (arctic bramble) a creeping thicket but unlike many brambles it has no prickles, leaves are three-lobed and toothed, flowers are bright red and are followed by dark red fruits, 15cm (6in) high; *R. illecebrosus* pinnate leaves that have autumn tints, and white flowers followed by mulberry-like fruits in late summer to autumn, 30cm (12in) high.

Features Spreading plants grown for their foliage, flowers and fruits.
Special Care Even these species may be invasive in a soil that is rich in nutrients, so they are better grown in poorer sites.
Propagation Take semi-ripe cuttings in summer or detach rooted pieces in winter.
Problems Grey mould.

Sagina Pearlwort

❝ *Saginas looks less like pearls and more like moss - with which the native species are very often confused. I suppose if moss could be transplanted and grown in your alpine garden, it would do the job just as well, and perhaps wouldn't have quite the same propensity to establish successfully and then turn a most unpleasant brown in the centre.* ❞

Origin S. *boydii* Scotland, S. *subulata* var. *glabrata* 'Aurea' Europe.
Habit Mat or cushion-forming, semi-evergreen or evergreen perennials.
Flowering Season Summer, but flowers insignificant.
Size S. *boydii* 3 x 8cm (1¼ x 3in), S. *subulata* var. *glabrata* 'Aurea' 1 x 20cm (½ x 8in).
Site Full sun with some shade at midday, or partial shade, and light, fairly poor soil.
Best Grown S. *boydii* is best in an alpine house, S. *subulata* var. *glabrata* 'Aurea' may be grown outdoors in a rock garden or between paving.

Features Grown for their foliage.
Special Care None.
Propagation Detach rosettes of S. *boydii* in early summer and grow on as cuttings. Lift and divide S. *subulata* var. *glabrata* 'Aurea' in spring.

Sagina subulata 'Aurea'

Problems In an alpine house, aphids, red spider mite and dying off in the centre.

Salix Willow

6 6 Mainly because of our familiarity with large pollarded trees along river banks and large weeping trees in parks, we tend too easily to think of willows as big plants. Yet as you travel to colder latitudes, you will continue to find Salix species, and even when you have travelled beyond the tree line, they will be there in quantity. And lovely things they are, these prostrate, creeping arctic-alpine willows, especially in the spring, when their little furry catkins sit up like candles over a carpet of twiggy branches. 9 9

Features Male and female catkins are borne on separate plants, the male forms being more attractive. These slow-growing willows improve with age when their gnarled branches develop.
Special Care None.
Propagation Take hardwood cuttings in late autumn.
Problems Aphids, leaf beetles, willow scale.

Origin Europe, western Asia, North America.
Habit Slow-growing deciduous shrubs, some prostrate.
Flowering Season Spring.
Size Most carpeting types 3–10 x 30–40cm (1¼–4 x 12–16in).
Site Full sun or light shade and moist but well-drained soil; intolerant of drought.
Best Grown Outdoors, in a rock garden or large trough.

Salix serpyllifolia

Recommended Varieties
Salix 'Boydii' AGM very slow-growing female clone, a natural hybrid between *S. reticulata* and *S. lapponum* from the Scottish Highlands, gnarled bush with thick stems and small round grey leaves, 45 x 20cm (18 x 8in) but eventually reaches 60cm (24in) high; *S. fruticulosa* (syn. *S. fur-cata*) spreading, carpeting shrub with small glossy leaves and pretty purple catkins, 20cm x 1m (8in x 3ft); *S. herbacea* (least willow) carpeting species native to Europe and western Asia grown for its small bright yellow catkins, in soft moist soil it may grow with its branches underground and only its glossy rounded leaves showing, 10 x 30cm (4 x 12in); *S. reticulata* AGM dwarf prostrate willow with rooting stems, grown for its glossy green leaves that are heavily veined above and covered in white hairs beneath, upright yellow catkins with pink tips, slow growing and ideal in a damp rock garden or trough, 8 x 30cm (3 x 12in); *S. retusa* another prostrate willow with rooting stems but more invasive than *S. reticulata*, upright grey catkins with golden yellow stamens, 10 x 40cm (4 x 16in); *S. serpyllifolia* (thyme-leaved willow) similar to *S. retusa* but more compact, 3 x 30cm (1¼ x 12in).

Saponaria Soapwort

66 Many years ago, a colleague introduced me to Saponaria ocymoides *and gave me a rooted cutting which I planted in a hollow-wall bed, where it soon established and tumbled downwards every year like a little pink waterfall. My gardening friend has passed away but his* Saponaria *is there still, a happy reminder of our gardening times together. 99*

Saponaria ocymoides

Origin S. ocymoides southern Europe, S. pumilio Austria and Italy.
Habit Low-growing evergreen perennials.
Flowering Season Summer.
Size S. ocymoides 8 x 45cm (3 x 18in), S. pumilio 8 x 20cm (3 x 8in).
Site Full sun and acidic or neutral soil.
Best Grown Outdoors, in a rock garden.

Features Narrow leaves and flat, five-petalled flowers.
Special Care Cut S. ocymoides back hard after flowering to keep it compact.
Propagation Take semi-ripe cuttings in summer. S. ocymoides may be raised from seed sown outdoors in early summer.
Problems Slugs, snails.

Recommended Varieties
S. ocymoides (tumbling Ted, rock soapwort) AGM spreading mat with hairy, bright green leaves covered in pink flowers in summer, short-lived plant but self-seeds, ideal for tumbling over sunny banks but it can swamp other plants; S. pumilio (dwarf soapwort) compact tufts of long pointed leaves, the large pink-purple flowers with notched petals are often borne around the edge of the cushion, may be short lived.

Saxifraga

66 Saxifraga is perhaps the single most indispensable and unavoidable genus for any and every alpine garden. Among a huge number of species and varieties there must surely be a plant to please everyone. But it is a huge range and there are many others, in addition to my recommendations, that I am sure will be ideal. Those I have listed here are all plants that I have grown or have seen and admired in other collections, but do look carefully at the nature of the various sub-groups because the plants in each are strikingly different. 99

Features Various leaf forms and flat, star-shaped flowers.
Special Care Provide some protection from winter wet.
Propagation Lift and divide herbaceous perennials in spring. Detach rosettes and root as cuttings in late spring to early summer. Sow seed in autumn in a cold frame.
Problems Aphid, red spider mites, slugs, vine weevil.

Saxifraga paniculata var. baldensis

Origin Mountainous regions throughout the northern hemisphere.
Habit Small, hardy evergreen perennials that vary greatly in habit, although rosettes or cushions are common.
Flowering Season Mostly spring or summer.
Size Varies (see below).
Site Fairly intolerant of shade but also liable to be damaged by direct hot sun. Neutral or alkaline soil.
Best Grown Outdoors, in a rock garden, or in an alpine house.

Recommended Varieties

There are many botanical groups in the genus Saxifraga but, for gardening purposes they may conveniently be reduced to four. Different plants in different groups sometimes have the same name, however, so check when buying. The following is a very small selection of the many available.

Encrusted and silver saxifrages Leaves encrusted with beads of lime, best on alkaline soils, thrive in light shade and dry conditions: S. cochlearis rosettes form a cushion, white flowers in early summer, 25 x 15cm (10 x 6in), S. 'Minor' compact form of S. cochlearis only 10cm (4in) high, S. 'Southside Seedling' bright green rosettes, white flowers with red spots, 30 x 15cm (12 x 6in), S. 'Lutea' pale yellow; S. paniculata (syn. S. aizoon) silver-green rosettes, creamy white flowers in early summer, 15 x 25cm (6 x 10in), var. baldensis (syn. 'Baldensis') dwarf form with red-tinted flower stems, 10 x 15cm (4 x 6in), S. 'Rosea' shell pink; S. 'Tumbling Waters' silver-green rosettes form a hummock, white flowers in spring, 75 x 30cm (30 x 12in); S. 'Whitehill' violet tints on rosettes, heavy lime encrustation, creamy white flowers, 30 x 40cm (12 x 16in).

Mossy saxifrages Soft feathery, moss-like hummocks: S. 'Bob Hawkins' variegated leaves of green, cream and pink, white flowers in summer, 15 x 30cm (6 x 12in); S. 'Cloth of Gold' slow-growing rosettes of yellow leaves, white flowers, intolerant of dry spells and hot sun, 3–15 x 15cm (1¼–6 x 6in); S.

'Dartington Double' double white flowers; S. 'Elf' carmine, dwarf; S. 'Gaiety' deep pink flowers; S. 'White Pixie' pure white flowers, dwarf.

Kabschia or Porophyllum saxifrages Sometimes called cushion saxifrages, rosettes or leafy shoots often with lime encrustations, slow-growing plants flowering from late winter to early spring: S. 'Boston Spa' bright green cushions, yellow flowers, 4 x 20cm (1½ x 8in); S. 'Buttercup' slow-growing, glossy rosettes, bright yellow flowers, 6 x 6cm (2½ x 2½in); S. 'Carmen' dull green cushion, yellow flowers, 5 x 15cm (2 x 6in); S. 'Cranbourne' (syn. 'Valborg', 'Valentine', S. x anglica 'Cranbourne') dark green rosettes, deep rose-pink flowers fading with age are borne in early summer, 4 x 10cm (1½ x 4in); S. 'Gloria' spiky cushion, white flowers, 8 x 8cm (3 x 3in); S. 'Gold Dust' golden-yellow flowers, 9 x 15cm (3½ x 6in); S. 'Gregor Mendel' (syn. S. x apiculata) glossy green cushion, primrose-yellow flowers, 15 x 30cm (6 x 12in); S. 'Haagii' dark green rosettes, golden-yellow flowers, 10 x 15cm (4 x 6in); S. 'Jenkinsae' dark green cushion, lilac-pink flowers, 5 x 7cm (2 x 2¾in); S. juniperifolia bright green cushion, prickly, sparse yellow flowers, 8 x 10cm (3 x 4in); S. 'Myra' very slow-growing rosettes form a dark green cushion, deep red-purple flowers in early spring, 2–5cm x 8–10cm (½–2 x 3–4in); S. 'Penelope' green cushion, amber flowers, 5 x 8cm (2 x 3in); S. 'Riverslea' grey-green leaves, rich claret flowers, 5 x 8cm (2 x 3in); S. 'Sulphurea' (syn. S. 'Moonlight')

grey-green mound of rosettes, sulphur-yellow flowers, 15 x 15cm (6 x 6in).

Other saxifrages S. 'Clarence Elliott' compact rosettes, rose-pink flowers in summer, 15 x 15cm (6 x 6in); S. ferdinandi-coburgi grey-green rosettes with golden-yellow flowers in spring, 8 x 10cm (3 x 4in); S. 'Flore Pleno'; S. fortunei (syn. S. cortusifolia var. fortunei) deciduous or semi-evergreen, mid-green leaves with purple tints, white flowers in late summer to autumn, 30 x 30cm (12 x 12in); S. oppositifolia dark green rosettes form a flat mat, pink, red-purple or white flowers in early summer, 3–5 x 20cm (1¼–2 x 8in); S. 'Ruth Draper', like S. oppositifolia but with large flowers of bright rose-pink; S. 'Wada' semi-evergreen, not hardy in cold winters but can thrive in sheltered woodland, lime-free soil and shade, glossy green leaves age to bronze-red, white flowers on red-brown stems in autumn, 30 x 30cm (12 x 12in); S. umbrosa prefers moist shade, leathery rosettes form a mat of dark green leaves, tiny white flowers with pink centres appear in early summer, 25 x 30cm (10 x 12in), var. primuloides neat, mid-green rosettes, white flowers with red spots in summer, 30 x 30cm (12 x 12in); S. x urbium thrives in moist shade, fleshy rosettes form a mat, pale pink flowers in early summer, spreads and can be invasive, 25 x 60cm (10 x 24in); S. 'Winifred Bevington' thrives in light soil and partial shade, white flowers with pink centres appear in early summer, 10 x 20cm (4 x 8in).

PERENNIALS AND SHRUBS

Sedum Stonecrop

❝ *I am always hesitant in recommending sedums as plants for the alpine garden in case someone forgets my precise suggestions and buys the wrong one, which will soon appear in many other parts of your garden, too. Stick to those that I have named and you will have some charming and colourful additions to your collection.* ❞

Origin Mountains of the northern hemisphere.
Habit Succulents of various sizes and shapes.
Flowering Season Summer to autumn.
Size 1–10 x 15–60cm (½–4 x 6–24in) to indefinite.
Site Most require a sunny site but a few tolerate partial shade, and *S. cauticola* is better in shade. Tolerant of most soils, even if poor and dry, although intolerant of cold, wet sites.
Best Grown Outdoors, in a trough.

Features Flat or cylindrical fleshy leaves and branched clusters of star-like flowers.
Special Care Cut back if plants threaten to swamp their neighbours.
Propagation Lift and divide plants in spring or autumn, or take cuttings of non-flowering shoots in spring. Sow seed of species in spring.
Problems Aphids, mealy bugs, root rots, vine weevil.

Recommended Varieties
Many sedums are invasive, but this is a small selection from the numerous species available that are usually more restrained: *S. cauticola* (syn. *Hylotelephium cauticolum*) AGM herbaceous perennial from Japan with an unkempt habit, creeping stems and fleshy blue-green foliage tinted with purple, useful late-flowering plant with pink-purple flowers in autumn, 10 x 30cm (4 x 12in), 'Lidakense' purple flowers and grey foliage; *S. ewersii* similar to *S. cauticola* but often later flowering, Himalayas and Mongolia; *S. kamtschaticum* AGM originates in eastern Siberia and northern China and thrives in partial shade, clump-forming semi-evergreen with glossy deep green leaves, pink buds open to golden-yellow flowers in late summer, 10 x 25cm (4 x 10in), var. *floriferum* 'Weihenstephaner Gold' lax, fleshy stems and mid-green leaves, numerous flowering shoots bear deep yellow flowers from summer until mid-autumn, 10 x 60cm (4 x 24in), var. *kamtschaticum* 'Variegatum' AGM has leaves with creamy-white margins; *S. spathulifolium* popular species from western North America, mat-forming evergreen with brittle stems and grey-green leaves, sprawling flower stems carry flat heads of yellow flowers, tolerates partial shade, 10 x 60cm (4 x 24in), 'Cape Blanco' (syn. 'Cappa Blanca') AGM white bloom on the leaves provides an effective contrast to the yellow flowers, protect from winter wet to prevent damage to the foliage and hope that the local blackbirds don't tear it to pieces, 'Purpureum' AGM foliage has a purple flush; *S. spurium* evergreen species from northern Iran and the Caucasus that forms a spreading, tangled mat, flower colour varies from white to various shades of pink, best on acidic soil in partial shade, 10 x 60cm (4 x 24in), there are a number of named varieties including var. *album* white-flowered form, 'Purpurteppich' (syn. 'Purple Carpet') compact form with purple foliage and dark purple-red flowers, 'Schorbuser Blut' (syn. 'Dragon's Blood') AGM one of the best forms with deep red flowers and purple-tinted green leaves, 'Variegatum' variegated foliage.

Sedum lidakense

Sempervivum
Houseleek

"Sempervivums are (I think) called houseleeks because they have a fondness for growing on house roofs, and because someone must have once thought they looked like leeks. But they might just as well have acquired the name because they have been popular for many years as house plants. This tells you something about them: that they can thrive in the dry conditions in our houses and also that they benefit from some shelter."

Origin Mountains of Europe and Asia.
Habit Small, rosette-forming evergreens.
Flowering Season Summer.
Size 3–8 x 20–30cm (1¼–3 x 8–12in).
Site Full sun and best in moderately fertile soil but will tolerate poorer conditions.
Best Grown Outdoors, in a rock garden, wall crevice or container; good plants for poor, dry, exposed places. Those that resent winter wet should be grown in an alpine house.

Features Colourful leaf rosettes and star-like flowers.
Special Care Soft-hairy species need protection from winter wet. Leaf rosettes die after flowering.
Propagation Sow seed in a cold frame in spring, or detach offsets and root them in spring or in early summer.
Problems Rust.

Recommended Varieties
A huge genus with numerous species, so the following are but a small selection. Note that, apart from the few named forms, there is also a huge number of 'varieties' and selections, each available from just a few suppliers: *S. arachnoideum* (cobweb houseleek) AGM light green to red rosettes with cobweb-like hairs so requires winter protection, rose-red flowers; *S. calcareum* species from the south-western Alps with blue-green leaf rosettes tipped purple-brown and with pale pink flowers; *S.* var. *ciliosum borisii* grey-green rosettes with red tints, a very hairy species with lemon-yellow flowers; *S. giuseppii* Spanish species, bright green rosettes with red tips and red flowers; *S. tectorum* (common houseleek) AGM wide rosettes that form large clumps of blue-green leaves with red-purple tints, and red-purple or deep pink flowers on hairy stems; *S. thompsonianum* small rosettes with red tints, sometimes yellow and pink flowers are produced, spreads to only 15cm (6in), requires winter protection.

Sempervivum ciliosum

PERENNIALS AND SHRUBS

Silene Campion

❝ Silene, *the campion, is a close relative of* Lychnis, *the catchfly (see p. 62), but without the sticky glandular hairs. Although there are tall-growing species, the alpine forms always seem to be typical alpines in their neat clump-forming, almost moss-like habit. They are easy to grow and should be among anyone's first alpine selection.* ❞

Origin Mostly Europe.
Habit Small perennials.
Flowering Season Early to late summer.
Size *S. acaulis* 5 x 20cm (2 x 8in), others 15–25 x 15–30cm (6–10 x 6–12in).
Site Full sun and neutral to alkaline soil.
Best Grown Outdoors, in a trough; those that resent winter wet should be grown in an alpine house.

Silene acaulis

Features Campion-like flowers.
Special Care None.
Propagation Sow seed in a cold frame in autumn; plants often self-seed once established. Root basal cuttings in spring.
Problems Outdoors, slugs and snails; in an alpine house, aphids, whitefly and red spider mite.

Recommended Varieties

Silene acaulis (moss campion) dwarf evergreen with a moss-like cushion of foliage, deep pink or white flowers with notched petals appear in summer, best grown on a scree, found in arctic Europe and Asia and European mountains, 'Mount Snowden' is a small, compact form; *S. alpestris* 'Flore Pleno' tufted evergreen with mid-green leaves and branching sprays of white, double flowers in summer; *S. elisabethae* (syn. *Melandrium elisabethae*) found on the limestone screes of the Italian Alps, semi-evergreen tuft of hairy leaves with large flowers of deep red-purple and two-lobed petals, requires protection from winter wet; *S. schafta* AGM semi-evergreen, clump-forming perennial from western Asia, bright green leaves and deep magenta, pink or white flowers with long tubes and notched petals, valuable plant as it flowers late; *S. uniflora* 'Robin Whitebreast' double-flowered form of a prostrate woody European coastal perennial, grey-green leaves and large white flowers with green calyx, rather like a small dianthus.

Sisyrinchium

❝ *Not everyone grows Sisyrinchium in their rock garden, as I do, but most people share my uncertainty over whether to call it a bulbous plant or an evergreen herbaceous perennial. Superficially, it could be mistaken for a small iris as the foliage is similar and they are indeed in the same family, but the flowers are certainly different and are especially appealing because they are present for much longer than iris flowers.* ❞

Features Iris-like foliage and star-like flowers.
Special Care Protect from excessive winter wet.
Propagation Most self-seed freely,

Sisyrinchium californicum

but plants may also be lifted and divided in early spring.
Problems Root rot.

Origin North and South America.
Habit Perennials, some semi-evergreen.
Flowering Season Early to late summer.
Size Heights vary from 12cm (5in) to 60cm (24in), but all have a spread of around 15cm (6in).
Site Full sun and neutral to slightly alkaline soil; succeeds well on poor soils.
Best Grown Outdoors, in a rock or gravel garden.

Recommended Varieties
It is always best to buy sisyrinchiums personally so you can see exactly what you are getting, as they masquerade under a bewildering variety of synonyms: *Sisyrinchium angustifolium* (syn. *S. bermudiana*, *S. birameun*; blue-eyed grass) semi-evergreen forming tufts with small but intense violet-blue flowers in summer, self-seeds freely, 20–50 x 15cm (8–20 x 6in); *S. californicum* (syn. *S. boreale*) semi-evergreen species from the western United States with grey-green leaves and bright yellow flowers, only barely hardy, tolerating down to -5°C (23°F), short lived but self-seeds freely, 60 x 15cm (24 x 6in), Brachypus Group (syn. *S. brachypus*) shorter form from northern America; *S. idahoense* 'Album' (syn. 'May Snow'), similar to *S. angustifolium* but a more dwarf form with white flowers, 12 x 15cm (5 x 6in).

Soldanella Snowbell

❝ *Cross a small bluebell with a snowdrop (in your mind's eye, not literally) and you end up with a snowbell, and one of the loveliest and least widely grown little alpines. When indeed their flowering time does coincide with the snow, their blue-purple bell-shaped flowers are especially enchanting.* ❞

Features Rounded or kidney-shaped leaves and bell-shaped flowers with fringed edges.

Soldanella alpina

Special Care Provide overhead protection in winter to obtain the best flowers.
Propagation Sow ripe seed and leave in a cold frame over winter. Plants may also be lifted and divided in early spring.
Problems Slugs, snails.

Origin Mountains of central and southern Europe.
Habit Evergreen, rosette-forming perennials.
Flowering Season Spring.
Size 12–15 x 12–15cm (5–6in x 5–6in), except *S. montana* 30 x 20cm (12 x 8in).
Site Sun or partial shade and cool, moist soil.
Best Grown Outdoors, in a rock garden or acidic-soil bed, or in an alpine house.

Recommended Varieties
Soldanella alpina (alpine snowbell) dainty clump-forming perennial with thick, dark green leaves, flowers are violet or violet-blue but this species can be reluctant to flower, 12 x 12cm (5 x 5in); *S. carpatica* AGM species from the western Carpathians that is similar to *S. alpina* but its leaves have purple undersides and the flowers are produced more freely, 12 x 12cm (5 x 5in); *S. hungarica* more vigorous form of *S. alpina* but with smaller flowers and often purple undersides to the leaves; *S. montana* larger species that grows to form a mound of bright green leaves and has fringed flowers of lavender-blue.

Tanacetum

❝ *The most familiar* Tanacetum, *especially to migraine sufferers, is feverfew, whose leaves effect a cure for some people. I don't think the leaves of the alpine species have any such properties, but they are certainly very good to look at and very delicately provide a foil for the little daisy flowers.* ❞

Tanacetum densum **subsp.** *amani*

Origin Turkey.
Habit Woody evergreen perennials.
Flowering Season Summer.
Size 25 x 20cm (10 x 8in).
Site Full sun in a sheltered position and well-drained soil.
Best Grown Outdoors, in a wall crevice, on a scree or in a raised bed.

Features Finely divided foliage and daisy or button-like flowers.

Special Care A well-drained site is essential.
Propagation Sow seed in warmth in late winter or early spring. Lift and divide plants or take basal cuttings, both in spring.
Problems None.

Recommended Varieties
Tanacetum densum spreading species grown mainly for its finely divided, silver-grey foliage, flowers are yellow but are rather insignificant; *T. haradjanii* is similar but with ray florets on the flowers.

Teucrium Germander

❝ *Germander sounds like a plant from Germany; it isn't. In reality, it means something rather similar to 'Chamae-' (see p. 32) except that it originates in Greek, not Latin. It means a low-growing oak tree. Admittedly, it takes a quantum leap of imagination to confuse a* Teucrium *with a* Quercus, *but they are certainly low growing and a bit woody.* ❞

Origin Mediterranean.
Habit Evergreen sub-shrubs.
Flowering Season Mostly early to late summer.
Size 8-20 x 20-30cm (3-8 x 8-12in).
Site Full sun in a warm, sheltered site and best on poorer soils.
Best Grown Outdoors, in a rock garden, except for barely hardy forms which should be grown in an alpine house.

Features Unusual flowers with a prominent lower lip of five lobes and no upper lip, plus aromatic foliage.
Special Care None.
Propagation Take semi-ripe cuttings in mid- to late summer.
Problems None.

Recommended Varieties
Teucrium ackermannii Turkish species that forms mat of grey-green foliage and has crimson-violet flowers from mid- to late summer; *T. aroanium* evergreen sub-shrub from rocky mountains of southern Greece with branching hairy stems, leaves are green with hairy undersides, in late summer to early autumn purple-grey flowers are borne in dense heads; *T. chamaedrys* (wall germander) sub-shrub with a wide distribution in Europe and western Asia that is very variable in habit, bears glossy oak-like leaves and pale to deep purple flowers from early summer into autumn, for the best shape and most flowers, grow in dry soil; *T. montanum* (mountain germander) spreading sub-shrub forming a tangled mat that should be cut back regularly, deep green leathery leaves with white undersides, from late spring to late summer produces flat heads of yellow-white flowers surrounded by a ruff of leaves; *T. pyrenaicum* (Pyrenean germander), as its name suggests this species comes from the Pyrenees, it forms a creeping semi-evergreen mat of slender stems with woolly leaves, from early to late summer there are flat heads of cream, mauve or bicoloured flowers.

Thymus 'Doone Valley'

Teucrium chamaedrys

Thymus Thyme

" *There are so many places in gardens where thymes are appropriate: but it is in the rock garden that you can grow whatever species take your fancy without having to worry if they taste good or will tolerate being trodden on.* "

Features Small but aromatic leaves and small, tubular, two-lipped flowers.
Special Care None.
Propagation Take semi-ripe cuttings in late summer.
Problems None, but it is worth replacing plants with cuttings every three years or so.

Origin Europe and Asia, usually on alkaline soils.
Habit Creeping or bushy evergreen perennials.
Flowering Season Summer.
Size Prostrate forms around 5 x 25–30cm (2 x 10–12in), shrubby types 25 x 25cm (10 x 10in) unless otherwise stated.

Site Full sun; particularly successful in alkaline gardens and unsatisfactory on heavy, cold sites.
Best Grown Outdoors, prostrate types may be used for softening the appearance of paving and paths and, as they are tolerant of being trampled, release their aroma when crushed underfoot.

Recommended Varieties
Thymus caespititius (syn. *T. azoricus*) Spanish species that grows to form a neat bush, bright green leaves and purple to pale pink flowers in late summer; *T.* x *citriodorus* (lemon-scented thyme) rather unkempt shrub with pale pink flowers, better named varieties include 'Aureus' AGM golden foliage, 'Bertram Anderson' (syn. *T.* 'Anderson's Gold') AGM grey-green leaves marked with gold, 'Silver Queen' creeping habit with irregular silver markings on the leaves; *T. doerfleri* species from Albania, very much like *T. serpyllum* but forming a carpet of hairy leaves and clusters of pink flowers, 15 x 45cm (6 x 18in); *T.* 'Doone Valley' shrubby habit, dark green leaves with yellow markings, purple-pink flowers, 10 x 20cm (4 x 8in); *T. serpyllum* (creeping thyme, wild thyme) the European wild thyme with dark green leaves and purple or white flowers, 15 x 30cm (6 x 12in), good named varieties include 'Albus' white flowers, 'Annie Hall' pink flowers, 'Pink Chintz' AGM grey-green leaves, clusters of small pink flowers; *T. vulgaris* 'Silver Posie' form of garden thyme that makes a neat bush, with white margins on the leaves and small white flowers, the best culinary variety.

PERENNIALS AND SHRUBS

Veronica Speedwell

❝ *I have already described the woody veronicas, the hebes (see p. 52); here we have their herbaceous counterparts. All are delightful, but don't make the mistake that alpine gardeners have made in the past of thinking that a pretty, creeping species from the Caucasus would make an appropriate addition. It is called* Veronica filiformis, *and it wouldn't – as a million owners of blue lawns will testify.* ❞

Origin Mostly Europe.
Habit Perennials with a mat-like habit, all those recommended below are evergreen.
Flowering Season Early to late summer.
Size Varies within the range 5–25 x 20–60cm (2–10 x 8–24in).
Site Sunny, with shelter from cold winds; tolerant of most soils but best on light, alkaline sites.
Best Grown Outdoors, in a rock garden or trough, or in an alpine house.

Veronica austriaca subsp. *teucrium* 'Crater Lake Blue'

Features Spikes of tubular flowers.
Special Care Lift and divide every two to three years to keep plants growing strongly. Dead-head regularly.
Propagation Lift and divide plants in autumn or spring. Species may be raised from seed sown in early spring.
Problems Powdery mildew, downy mildew, leaf spots.

Recommended Varieties
Veronica austriaca subsp. *teucrium* evergreen mat with upright stems and spikes of clear blue flowers from early to midsummer, provide winter cover in cold wet areas, 25 x 60cm (10 x 24in), 'Crater Lake Blue' AGM neat, mound-forming plant of rather good colour; *V. fruticans* (syn. *V. saxatilis*; rock speedwell) British native, also found throughout Europe, forms a neat evergreen mat and has deep blue flowers with a red eye, 8 x 20cm (3 x 8in); *V. nummularia* (Pyrenean speedwell) evergreen, mat-like species from damp rocky screes in France and Spain, small fleshy leaves and clusters of blue or pink flowers, 5–15 x 30cm (2–6 x 12in); *V. prostrata* (syn. *V. rupestris*; prostrate speedwell) AGM easy-to-grow evergreen species from Europe and western Asia, forms a mat with pale to deep blue flower spikes but may be too invasive for rock gardens, many named varieties available including 'Spode Blue' with pale blue flowers, 10–25 x 45cm (4–10 x 18in); *V. wormskjoldii* (syn. *V. stelleri*) native of Japan, forms a mat with purple-blue flowers from mid- to late summer, 10 x 25–30cm (4 x 10–12in).

Viola Pansy, violet

❝ *Of course, we all grow pansies, violets or violas and love them dearly. The majority of us, however, restrict ourselves to the pansy end of the spectrum, making use especially of the wonderful winter-flowering universals. But, in doing so, let's not forget the multiplicity of* Viola *species – nor that one or two of them will run riot given half a chance.* ❞

Features Heart-shaped or divided leaves and flat, five-petalled flowers.
Special Care Dead-head to promote further flowering. Some self-seed.
Propagation Take basal cuttings in midsummer or sow seed in spring.
Problems Mosaic virus, rust.

Recommended Varieties

A large genus, so the following is just a small selection of the small species available: *Viola biflora* (yellow wood violet) found in damp, shady mountain habitats, a creeping plant with pale green leaves and small bright yellow flowers in summer, 8 x 20cm (3 x 8in); *V. cornuta* (horned pansy) AGM native to the Pyrenees, an easy-to-grow but spreading species, the scented flowers are violet or lilac with a white eye and have a characteristic long spur behind the flower, they last from early summer to early autumn, 15 x 40cm (6 x 16in), Alba Group a white-flowered form, Lilacina Group has lilac-blue flowers, 'Minor' AGM dwarf form with white or lavender-blue flowers, only 7 x 20cm (2¾ x 8in) so ideal for rock gardens; *V. jooi* species from Romania

with scented pink or mauve flowers in late spring to midsummer, only 8 x 15cm (3 x 6in) tall; *V. lutea* (syn. *V. lutea* subsp. *elegans*; mountain pansy) widely distributed species from central and southern Europe, a creeping evergreen whose summer flowers have a short spur, flower colour varies from yellow, through blue, red and violet to white, and as it self-seeds freely these are commonly all found together, 7–15 x 7–15cm (2¾–6 x 2¾–6in); *V. odorata* (sweet violet) although often called the English violet this species is widely distributed in Europe, grown for its scented violet or white flowers with a short spur, which appear from late winter to early summer, self-seeds freely, there are many named varieties including 'Alba' a white-flowered form, 20 x 30cm (8 x 12in).

Origin Widely distributed, but most of those recommended below are from Europe.

Habit Clump-forming herbaceous perennials.

Flowering Season Varies (see below).

Size Varies, but most within the range 5–15 x 20–30cm (2–6 x 8–12in).

Site Sun or partial shade, thriving in most types of soil but may be less successful in soil where pansies or violas have been grown repeatedly in the past.

Best Grown Outdoors, in a trough.

Viola gracilis 'Lutea'

Waldsteinia

❝ Waldsteinia *always sounds to me like something out of a low-budget horror film. This is a great pity, because for many years the name coloured my judgement of what is in reality a most charming, if slightly vigorous, yellow-flowered ground cover plant. And the significance of that name? It commemorates an Austrian botanist called Count Franz Adam Waldstein von Wartenburg, who I am sure was utterly charming and never filed his teeth.* ❞

Features Leaves like those of a strawberry plant and saucer-shaped flowers.

Special Care Plants spread by runners so may be invasive.

Propagation Lift and divide plants in spring or autumn.

Problems None.

Waldsteinia ternata

Origin *W. fragarioides* eastern United States, *W. ternata* eastern Europe, China and Japan.

Habit Rhizomatous semi-evergreen perennials.

Flowering Season *W. fragarioides* late spring to early summer, *W. ternata* mid- to late spring.

Size 10 x 60cm (4 x 24in).

Site Partial or full shade, thriving in all except dry soils.

Best Grown Outdoors, rather invasive for rock gardens but useful as ground cover.

Recommended Varieties

Waldsteinia fragarioides very similar to *W. ternata* (below), but a taller plant with smaller flowers; *W. ternata* vigorous spreading plant, ideal for woodland conditions, offers fresh foliage for most of the year and bright yellow flowers in spring.

Crocus

" *The big, bold, orange, purple and white Dutch hybrid crocuses that scatter colour across many a municipal park in spring are all right in their way. But they are just too big and bold for the rock garden. Search among the species and varieties that are sold in small, select and discrete packets rather than the giant corms that you can shovel home in bulk, and you will find some treasures indeed. You will find plants that flower over many more months, too.* "

Origin Widespread, those recommended below are from Europe or the Middle East.

Habit Dwarf corm-forming perennials.

Flowering Season Varies with species (see below).

Size Most 5–10 x 3–5cm (2–4 x 1¼–2in).

Site Full sun unless otherwise stated; most species recommended below are best in a relatively poor, well-drained soil.

Best Grown Outdoors, in a rock garden, raised bed, trough or naturalized in grass. May also be grown very successfully in an alpine house.

Features Most species have goblet-shaped flowers and thin, grassy foliage.

Special Care Plant corms 8–10cm (3–4in) deep under a layer of fine-mesh chicken wire to deter mice and voles.

Propagation Sow ripe seed and keep the seedlings in a cold frame for two years before planting out. Small corms may also be removed from plants any time during the dormant period and replanted.

Problems Mice and voles may eat corms, and birds often attack the flowers. The vole problem can be solved by planting the corms slightly deeper and laying chicken wire over them.

Left: Crocus chrysanthus **'Blue Pearl'**
Below: Crocus **'Whitewell Purple'**

Recommended Varieties

Crocus angustifolius (syn. *C. susianus*; cloth of gold crocus) AGM spring-flowering species from southern Ukraine and Armenia, grown for its orange-yellow flowers marked with bronze, 5 x 5cm (2 x 2in); *C. banaticus* AGM species from north-eastern former Yugoslavia, Romania and south-western Ukraine, early autumn-flowering crocus with large lilac to purple flowers that open wide, slow to bulk up and best raised from seed, thrives in partial shade and moist but well-drained soil, 10 x 5cm (4 x 2in); *C. cartwrightianus* 'Albus' AGM crocus from Greece that flowers in autumn and early winter, best in an alpine house as it requires a warm, very well-drained site, the scented white flowers are goblet-shaped; *C. chrysanthus* from Turkey and the Balkans, almost invariably grown as one of the following fine spring-flowering varieties: 'Blue Pearl' AGM blue flowers with a yellow throat, 'Cream Beauty' AGM cream flowers with yellow throat, 'Ladykiller' AGM white flowers with deep purple outside, 'Zwanenburg Bronze' AGM yellow flowers with dark red-brown outside; *C. medius* AGM species from France and Italy with late-autumn flowers of a vivid purple with bright orange styles; *C. ochroleucus* AGM species from Syria, Lebanon and Israel, best grown in an alpine house as prone to winter weather damage, creamy white flowers with yellow throats appear in late autumn; *C. speciosus* AGM autumn-flowering crocus found in Turkey, Iran and central Asia, the flowers are various shades of blue and violet with deep purple or blue veins and much-divided orange styles, self-seeds readily and can be allowed to naturalize in grass, taller than most at 10–15cm (4–6in); *C. tommasinianus* AGM very popular and easy-to-grow species that flowers in late winter to early spring, slender flowers in shades of silver-lavender to red-purple are usually fairly weather tolerant, 'Whitewell Purple' has red-purple flowers with silver-mauve insides, and self-seeds readily; *C. tournefortii* AGM species from southern Greece best grown in an alpine house, the long-tubed flowers open wide and appear from late autumn to winter, flowers are pale lilac with much-divided orange styles and white anthers.

Crocus speciosus

BULBS

Galanthus Snowdrop

> *I've said on many occasions that snowdrops wouldn't have a chance in the summer garden when there are so many bigger and bolder things to take your eye. But that is exactly the point: they don't flower in summer, they flower in late winter and very often at a time before the bulk of the rock garden flowers have dared to unfold their buds.*

Origin Europe to western Asia.
Habit Small bulbous perennials.
Flowering Season Winter.
Size 10–15 x 5–10cm (4–6 x 2–4in).
Site Partial shade and moist but well-drained soil.
Best Grown Outdoors, in a rock garden or trough.

Features Pendent white flowers and narrow leaves.
Special Care None.
Propagation Lift and divide clumps of bulbs when the leaves start to die down; re-establishment from dormant bulbs is much more difficult. Sow ripe seed and keep in a cold frame over winter and then until it germinates.

Snowdrops hybridize readily and plants raised from seed may not come true.
Problems Narcissus bulb fly, grey mould.

Recommended Varieties
Galanthus caucasicus AGM species thought to have originated from Turkey and now considered to be a variant of *G. elwesii*, variable with broad glaucous leaves and a flowering display that lasts from late autumn to early spring, each flower has a green mark at the tip of each inner tepal; *G. elwesii* AGM glaucous species from Turkey and the Balkans that produces scented flowers in late winter, there are two green markings on each inner tepal; *G. ikariae* species from Turkey and the Aegean Islands, bright green leaves, flowers in late winter to early spring, the tip of each inner tepal is marked with green; *G.* 'Lady Beatrix Stanley' grown for its double flowers that are 2.5cm (1in) across, each inner tepal has a tiny green mark, glaucous foliage; *G. nivalis* (common snowdrop) AGM the familiar snowdrop that is found over a wide area from the Pyrenees to the Ukraine and although widespread in Britain is not thought to be native, small but valued for its winter flowers and glaucous foliage, the best species for naturalizing, there are many good named varieties including 'Flore Pleno' AGM a sterile double-flowered form that may be increased by offsets, and 'Viridapicis' which has a very long spathe, sometimes split in two, and green marks on the inner tepals.

Galanthus nivalis 'Flore Pleno'

Iris

*Iris '**J.S. Dijt**'*

66 Not many bulbous plants engender so many admiring gasps as the dwarf bulbous irises that follow snowdrops and accompany some of the spring crocuses. There is something very special about such rich regal colours on such small and beautifully proportioned flowers. 99

Features Slender iris flowers on a small scale.

Special Care After flowering the leaves lengthen and the plants should then be fed with a liquid fertilizer high in potash. The bulbs are dormant over the summer, when they should be kept just moist.

Propagation Separate bulb offsets in early summer.

Problems Slugs, snails, ink spot fungus.

Origin *I. reticulata* Turkey and Caucasus.
Habit All those recommended below are bulbous reticulata types.
Flowering Season Late winter to early spring.
Size 10–15cm in flower (4–6in).
Site Full sun and well-drained neutral or slightly alkaline soil.
Best Grown Outdoors, in a trough or raised bed.

Recommended Varieties
Iris 'Cantab' pale blue flowers with yellow markings, 'Harmony' royal-blue flowers with yellow markings, 'J. S. Dijt' red-purple flowers with orange markings, ' Katharine Hodgkin' pale blue flowers marked with yellow and blue veins, *I. reticulata* has fragrant flowers in various shades of blue, violet or purple, all with central yellow markings.

Iris reticulata

BULBS

Narcissus Daffodil

❛❛ *Even away from the rock garden, I think that gardeners tend to choose* Narcissus *varieties (and daffodils especially) that are far too big. The scaled-down plants, whether true species or cultivated varieties, are much more in proportion to domestic gardens – and much less prone to damage from wind and rain.* ❜❜

Recommended Varieties

Narcissus asturiensis (syn. *N. minimus*) species from Portugal and Spain with pale yellow flowers in late winter to early spring; *N. bulbocodium* (hoop-petticoat daffodil) widespread distribution in Europe and northern Africa, foliage begins to appear in autumn but the unusual funnel-shaped flowers of deep yellow not until mid-spring, good for naturalizing in damp grass that dries out in summer, var. *conspicuus* has the finest flowers; *N. cantabricus* subsp. *cantabricus* (white hoop-petticoat daffodil), similar to *N. bulbocodium* except the flowers are white, best grown in an alpine house;

N. cyclamineus AGM species from Portugal and Spain with golden-yellow flowers in early spring, unusual-shaped flowers with swept-back petals and a long narrow corona; *N.* 'Hawera' has several flowering stems per bulb, making this a good choice for small containers, the flowers are golden yellow and appear in late spring, 'Jack Snipe' white flowers with yellow trumpets in early to mid-spring, a long-flowering variety, 'Minnow' small tazetta type with pale yellow flowers in mid-spring, 'Peeping Tom' cyclamineus type with golden yellow flowers, one of the earliest to flower, 'Pipit' scented lemon-yellow flowers in mid- to late spring.

Origin Species from Europe and northern Africa, but many varieties are of garden origin.
Habit Bulbous perennials.
Flowering Season Spring.
Size Varies, the small types 8–25cm (3–10in) high.
Site Sun or partial shade and moist soil.
Best Grown Outdoors, in a rock garden or large trough.

Features Strap-like leaves and trumpet flowers.
Special Care Feed after flowering with a high-potash feed. Do not cut back the foliage until at least six weeks after flowering.
Propagation Sow ripe seed of the species in a cold frame. Lift and divide offsets as the leaves fade.
Problems Slugs, fungal rots, narcissus fly, viruses.

Tulipa Tulip

❛❛ *If large, cup-shaped flowers on tall stems are what tulips mean to you, then you are missing a great deal of gardening pleasure – and you are missing some superb rock garden plants. Most of the numerous species tulips have very short stems and a squat habit. They are also much more reliably perennial than their large-flowered hybrid relatives and I still think the true, unaltered species are the most beautiful of all.* ❜❜

Narcissus bulbocodium var. conspicuus

Features Long leaves and goblet-shaped or star-like flowers.
Special Care Dead-head and remove any fallen leaves after flowering.
Propagation Seed may be sown when ripe and kept in a cold frame, but it can be many years before flowers are produced. Bulbs may be lifted in the summer and the offsets separated.
Problems Slugs, eelworms, rots.

Origin Hot, dry regions of temperate Europe, Asia and the Middle East.
Habit Bulbous perennials.
Flowering Season Early to mid-spring unless otherwise stated.
Size 15–30cm (6–12in) high unless otherwise stated.
Site Full sun and soil that is fertile but well drained; better when dry over the summer.
Best Grown Outdoors in a rock garden or large trough, or in an alpine house or bulb frame.

Tulipa turkestanica

Recommended Varieties
Tulipa biflora (syn. *T. polychroma*) species from Turkey and Iran with grey-green leaves and scented, star-like white flowers with a red margin and yellow centres, appearing from late winter to spring, 10cm (4in); *T. clusiana* var. *chrysantha* (syn. *T. chrysantha*) AGM bowl-shaped yellow flowers with red or brown outsides in early to mid-spring; *T. humilis* species from Turkey and Iran with grey-green leaves and star-shaped flowers in early to mid-spring, flowers vary in colour from pale pink to purple-pink or magenta, often with green or black markings, Violacea Group (syn. *T. vio-lacea*) violet flowers; *T. kaufmanniana* (water-lily tulip) bowl-shaped variable flowers in early to mid-spring that may be cream, yellow, pink, orange or red and often have a flush of pink or green; *T. kolpakowskiana* AGM bowl-shaped yellow flowers with red, orange or green markings; *T. linifolia* AGM grey-green leaves with red wavy margins, bowl-shaped red flowers with black-purple marks at the base, Batalinii Group 'Bright Gem' AGM soft warm yellow flowers with a beige or biscuit flush, Batalinii Group 'Bronze Charm' orange-bronze flowers; *T. orphanidea* Whittallii Group (syn. *T. whittallii*) species from Bulgaria, Greece and Turkey with star-shaped flowers and narrow, upright foliage in early to mid-spring, flowers are orange with a green tint on the outer petals; *T. tarda* AGM very widely grown species from central Asia with bright green leaves and star-like flowers that are white with a yellow centre, self-seeds very freely; *T. turkestanica* AGM species from north-western China, star-like white flowers with a green flush on the outside of the flower and a yellow centre; *T. urumiensis* AGM delicate-looking species from Iran, star-shaped yellow flowers with lilac-flushed or red-brown outsides and more or less prostrate foliage.

INDEX

PHOTOGRAPHIC ACKNOWLEDGEMENTS

Andrew Lawson Front Cover
Garden Picture Library/John Glover Back Cover
A–Z Botanical Collection 25, /Andrew Brown 61 right,
/Michael Chandler 43 bottom/Michael R. Chandler 77,
/Bob Gibbons 36, 63, 86 right, /J.M. Hirst 73, /Jiri Loun 49,
/Maurice Nimmo 70 bottom, /Annie Poole 70 top, 82 left,
/J. Brunaden Rapkins 80, /Chris Wheeler 68
Garden Picture Library 8, /Philippe Bonduel 84, /Chris
Burrows 82 right, /Linda Burgess 27, /Rex Butcher 55,
/Brian Carter 46, /Erika Craddock 6, /Eric Crichton 1
bottom, 66, /David England 20, /Vaughan Fleming 64, /John
Glover 4, 7 top, 52 left, 61 left, 74, 88 top, /Sunniva Harte
56 right, 85 right, /Neil Holmes 31, 44, 62 top, 93, /Jane
Legate 15, /Jerry Pavia 50, 85 left, /Howard Rice 2, 39, 40,
48, 67, 91 bottom, /J.S. Sira 51 Bottom, 88 Bottom, /Nicky
White 37
John Glover 29
Octopus Publishing Group Ltd. 1 top, 2-3, 13 top, 23,
26, 28, 30, 34, 42, 57, 58 right, 71, 81
Harpur Garden Library 9, 11, 14 top, 35, 41, 51 top,
56 left, 75, 76, 91 top, 92
Andrew Lawson 10, 13 bottom, 21, 33 right, 45, 52
right, 53, 60, 62 bottom, 65 top, 65 bottom, 69, 72 right,
78 left, 83, 86 left, 87, 89, 90
Photos Horticultural 5, 7 bottom, 12, 14 bottom, 16,
17, 18, 58 left, 72 left, 78 right
Harry Smith Collection 22, 33 left, 38, 43 top, 47, 54